THE DYNAMICS
OF SUCCESS
MOTIVATION

THE DYNAMICS OF SUCCESS MOTIVATION

Inspiring you to greatness

—❦—

KENNETH W KHRISTIAN

First Edition
ISBN: 0999339508
ISBN-13: 9780999339503
Library of Congress Control Number: 2017916362
Promote Health America, Smyrna, GA

DEDICATION

This book is dedicated to my mother, who passed away in November 2007. I thank you for all you did for me and all the things you tried to do but were unable to accomplish. I salute you for your relentless courage in facing life's adversities and for your hard work in providing for my brothers and me. I wish you were here to see the first copy of my book. Also to my grandmother, who passed away in December 2002. I'd like to take this opportunity to thank you for doing for me all the things my mother was unable to do, most of all for the genuine love you showed and all the positive inspiration and motivation. I saw you do extraordinary things with the little you had to do them with. You were my pathway for believing in God and me.

I always love, thank, and appreciate both of you. I wish you were here to celebrate this accomplishment milestone with me.

APPRECIATION

SPECIAL THANKS TO PROFESSOR RICHARD A. Cross for helping me and making this book possible. Your knowledge, wisdom, and expertise have been extremely valuable, and I appreciate it very much. To all my coworkers and friends who encourage me not to give up on my goals and dreams, I thank you all for your inspiration and motivation.

CONTENTS

INTRODUCTION

———⚬⚬⚬———

I WOULD LIKE TO THANK you for taking the time out of your day to pick up this book. I truly believe you will find something in this book that will benefit you in some way. This book provides **twelve Master Strategies to help turn your goals and dreams into reality** by which you will be able to unlock your capacities for health, happiness, success, well-being, and creativity.

With the simple and practical strategies, I have provided here, you will find that you already have what it takes to be successful. You may not agree with everything in this book, and that's OK. Some of you may not like this book at all, and that's still OK. For those of you who can see the value of this book, I hope that you not only read it but also apply what you learn from this book and make the strategies a part of your life. From my personal experience, I would like to say that you can make your goals and dreams a reality. It's possible. It will require some effort on your part, but if you put the strategies in this book into practice and apply them to your lifestyle, you'll dramatically increase your chances of becoming successful. What I suggest you do is learn all the strategies in this book and use them to build your own pyramid of success. The strategies I share in this book will work together to make your journey to success dynamic. I would like to tell you about the three important concepts in this book. Those concepts are *foundation*, *formation*, and *leverage*. Some of the strategies will collaborate to form a firm foundation. Remember, a house cannot stand without a foundation, and neither does your success. Others will work together to develop formation.

You will use some to create leverage. I will share in this book all the things you need to make your dreams a reality. You deserve the absolute best that life has to offer. If you want to pursue the best for your life but aren't sure how to start, these strategies will help you manifest your dreams and set you on the fast track to success. The strategies are simple and practical. You may have heard of them before in different ways, and that's fine. I hope that hearing them again will help you to make them a part of your consciousness. I would like to introduce them in an easy and concise way, so you can incorporate them into your daily life right away.

I believe that when you begin to apply these twelve strategies to your life, you'll see a tremendous difference in what you can achieve this year, in three years, in five years, and beyond. It's one thing to acquire knowledge, but when you learn how to put knowledge into action so that it can benefit you, knowledge takes on a whole new meaning. Yes, take knowledge, apply it, and let it help you. You will gain the power to do anything you like to do and have anything you want. Make a commitment to change how you think about achieving your goals and dreams and being successful by learning these strategies. It's your choice; it always was and always will be.

—Ken Khristian

SUCCESS

———— ⊶⊷ ————

WHAT IS SUCCESS? SUCCESS IS the accomplishment of an aim or purpose. Success comes in all shapes, forms and sizes. It's a part of all professions and genres. It can be classified as personal, private, confidential or classified. It can be dynamic depending of the magnitude of its worth and value. For many people success has a time, purpose, place and passion.

There is a hierarchy of success, because everyone will not experience success on the same level. Success may mean surviving day to day for one person, while success for another person would mean taking their financial status from 6 figures to 7 figures. The real question is what success means to you. Success is believing in your own ability to make things happen and get something accomplished that will give you value and worth.

Success is having the courage to step out of your comfort zone and actively engage in something that will give your life purpose and meaning. Success is using desire to motivate and

xv

inspire you too truly strive for something great. Success is setting goals and diligently striving to make sure they happen. Success is using your imagination as a workshop to visualize your achievements. Success is being excellent in all your endeavors and anything you undertake. Success is not letting failure deter you from the things that will bring you joy and happiness in life. Success is doing what you love and loving what you do, knowing that it's all relative to being happy in life. Success is being honest to yourself and others, because it's a part of integrity. Success is understanding that life is beautiful, and you are the only opportunity to manifest your goals and dreams.

Success is taking 100 percent responsibility for your existence and never being complacent, conformed or codependent on anyone else for your happiness. Success is persisting to the bitter end, knowing that victory is worth the effort.

SUCCESS AFFIRMATIONS

* SUCCESS COMES TO ME.
* I GIVE MYSELF PERMISSION TO SUCCEED.
* I ACHIEVE INFINITE SUCCESS.
* MY MIND IS ABSOLUTELY FOCUSED ON SUCCESS.
* PEOPLE SEE ME AS CONFIDENT AND SUCCESSFUL.
* MY DREAMS WILL LEAD TO SUCCESS.
* I HAVE ABSOLUTE FAITH IN MY ABILITY TO SUCCEED.
* SUCCESS IS MINE TO ENJOY.
* I AM EXPERIENCING PHENOMENAL SUCCESS.
* I HAVE WHAT IT TAKE TO SUCCEED.
* I SURROUND MYSELF WITH SUCCESSFUL PEOPLE.
* I COMMIT TO CREATE A LIFESTYLE OF SUCCESS.

BELIEF

Belief is the knowledge that we can do something. It's the inner feeling that what we undertake, we can accomplish. For the most part, all of us have the ability to look at something and know whether or not we can do it. So, in belief there is power: our eyes are opened; our opportunities become plain; our visions become realities.

—MOTIVATIONAL QUOTES

Belief

———∞∞∞———

LET ME TAKE THIS OPPORTUNITY and use some professional sport franchises to help stress a point about belief. Only 4 NFL teams the Pittsburgh Steelers, New England Patriots, Dallas Cowboys and the San Francisco 49ers have won the Super Bowl more than 4 times. The New York Yankees of the AL have played in more World Series. The most Series appearances, victories, and losses of any Major League Baseball franchise. Only 5 NBA teams Celtics, Lakers, Bulls, Spurs and Warriors have won the NBA Championships more than 3 times.

I use these professional sports teams as an example to illustrate and make a point of what belief can do for you. Belief makes success possible. You can succeed through belief. Do you believe it's possible?

Belief is a state or habit of mind in which trust or confidence is placed in some person or thing. A belief is a powerful concept: Although it's just a word, it has the power to help anyone manifest their destiny. Once you develop a belief system that supports your goals, you are empowered with the ability to create and manifest the things you desire. Yes, you become a powerful creator, because you can turn your thoughts into reality. Have you consciously created a belief system specifically for your personal use to help motivate and inspire you to achieve your goals and dreams? Whatever you believe now will have been established over time.

Belief is not just a word; it is a philosophy that holds magical powers. You'll hear most if not every successful person shares that having a strong belief system is a must to achieve success. The secret key to gain access to power is that you should intentionally activate your own internal power of belief. If you don't activate your own power of belief, it will remain dormant until you make a conscious effort to transform the ideology into a habitual thought pattern. Therefore, if there is something you want to believe about yourself or if you want to reprogram your mind to think differently, you may have to make it a part of your daily routine. This is what actively releases the power of the word *belief.*

By activating your belief within yourself in what you are trying to accomplish, not only will you have a strong conviction, but you'll be more optimistic. When you are optimistic you'll be more likely to have faith in what you believe. For example, I believe, without a reasonable doubt, that God exist, so this makes God a living entity in my reality. What I mean is this: I don't have to see what I believe to believe that it exists or it's possible. For me, believing is not seeing. For some people, they must see to believe, but the power of believing means that you have faith that something exists without it being seen by you physically.

When a person develops a belief system, they empower the creativity that lies within. Belief is the first step to laying a foundation to create abundance in our lives. The day we were born into this world, we embarked on a fantastic voyage of discovery called life. Life makes no promises and has no guarantees. However, if you build a belief system it can help you to enhance the quality of your life.

We were born to evolve, so this makes us dynamic; therefore, each of us has the power to choose. What will you choose? By the way, you may already know that human growth and development requires changes. So, to change into what you desire your belief system must match your desire.

A belief can be adopted from a wide variety of sources. As we grow up and develop, we acquire certain beliefs, some even unconsciously. What we believe is what we assume to be true. It's through our belief in what's possible that our goals and dreams will be manifested. Your belief needs to be solid. That means not wavering when things look uncertain. The environment in which we live plays a major role on how we form our beliefs. External factors help to condition us and influence our belief system.

Some beliefs are embedded in our genes, passed to us from our parents. Wherever you are on your journey, you may need to question your beliefs, especially if you keep doing things that do not serve your betterment.

If you were born into an environment of lack and limitations, you are more likely to be conditioned to have a mind-set of lack and limitations. Therefore, lack will become your default belief. What I mean by that is you'll be limiting yourself based on generational conditioning, or your firm belief will be that what you want is not possible. I would like to implore you to think beyond what you hold as true. How can you do that? You can do that by reprogramming your mind by reading books, listening to daily motivational and inspirational messages, and actively engaging in various things that will cause you to change your old way of thinking.

If you want to live a more motivated and inspirational life, the belief you hold on what's possible should be one of strong conviction. If you have strong conviction, you will not let go what you want to achieve when you are tested by life's trials. It's not a question of *if* you're going to be tested; you *are* going to be tested. Not believing in yourself will prevent you not from asking for help or even taking the first step. But as you may have already heard, "The journey of a thousand miles begins with a single step." Will you take that first step? Do you believe you can, despite where you started from?

If you want to change your perception about achievement, make it a habit in your mind. This means you constantly think in terms of what you want to achieve.

Once we develop a strong belief, we tend to stick to it for our lifetime, but beliefs can change over time. However, as time goes on and we learn more, we may develop a new belief system. Don't be afraid to challenge or redefine what you believe, especially if it will better help you understand the world you live in. Don't let your beliefs confine you mentally or psychologically because that will make it difficult for you to accept customs and beliefs from different cultures around the globe.

Remember, **"As a man thinketh so is he."** Our mental attitude is everything; it's all in your mind. How do you really feel about what you believe? Without doubting and second-guessing about yourself, do you truly believe that all things are possible? I remember days when I didn't even believe that I could write this book. Your brain has the power to navigate you to your destination. It starts with believing; you must develop a positive mental attitude about what you believe. Focus on the things you want to accomplish; keep them at the front of your thoughts. Use the power of your mind to help you manifest your goals and dreams.

Sometimes we undermine our own purpose by allowing a self-defeating mental attitude to overshadow our true happiness. Reprogram your mind for success. Reprogram the way you think by inputting new ideas into your thought process. That's something you have control over. Discard all thought processes that are hindering your success. These thoughts can include anger, bitterness, regrets, resentment, discontent etc. These thoughts will only make you regress in life. Suppress old thought processes with new thoughts that are positive; only feed your mind with what will motivate and inspire you to reach your goals. Don't let unnecessary thoughts defeat your purpose. Reprogram yourself to be a new person, and redesign yourself with the purpose of achieving success.

On your road to creating an abundant life (you do want an abundant life, right?), your belief is going to play an integral part in making your dreams come to fruition. I believe it's time for you to fulfill your destiny.

Don't delay in establishing your own belief system, because it is that important. It doesn't matter where you are on your journey: you have the power within yourself to reprogram your mind, so just do it. On your road to a better life, you must first believe that it is possible. The moment you carry this conviction, that the moment you will come closer too manifesting your goals and dreams into a reality. Your thoughts will become the reality. It's all in the mind, so relax, release, and let go.

I really want to drive home the importance of your belief system. The first and most important step to success is to truly believe you can succeed. Combine the energy force of your mind and body to form a powerful success mechanism that will fuel your determination. You can overcome and conquer any situation through mental toughness, so use your creative imagination to visualize your success.

Give your mind the resources it needs so that it can help you to create the things you want in your life. Don't let doubt limit your realization of abundance. The only thing that stands between you and what you want out of life is your faith to believe that it's possible and the will to make it happen.

Beliefs are important because behavior is important, and your behavior depends on your beliefs. Everything you do can be traced back to your beliefs and how you perceive the things around you. Brought together, beliefs and knowledge form a mental perception of the world around you: a belief about the world is the mental attitude that the world is structured in one way rather than another.

This means that beliefs are necessarily the foundation for action: whatever actions you take in the world around you are based on your mental representation of the world. If you believe something is true, you must be willing to act as if it is true. If you are unwilling to act as though it is true, you can't really claim to believe it.

Therefore, actions matter much more than words. You can't know the contents of a person's mind, but you can know if their actions are consistent with what they say they believe. A person might claim that they love their neighbors, but does their behavior reflect such love? Beliefs also help determine your reactions to others' behavior. This means that beliefs are not an entirely private matter.

In fact, beliefs you try to keep to yourself may influence your actions enough to become a matter of legitimate concern of others. Beliefs can cause harm directly by promoting or justifying harm toward others. These beliefs can include prejudice, bigotry, racism etc. Beliefs can cause harm indirectly by promoting controversial representations of what you believe. The real question is how much harm the beliefs might ultimately cause, either directly or indirectly.

If you want to succeed, you must first believe that you can. If you think it's possible, it's possible; if you don't think it's possible, it won't be possible. It depends on how you think about the situation. You are the only person standing in your way, so believe that it's possible and make it happen. Once you carry unwavering energy, determination, and faith, your dreams will become a reality. In the end, the common denominator for success in whatever you attempt to accomplish is having faith and belief that it's possible. You are what you think and believe. You can look at any situation and know if you can do it.

Don't let doubt keep you from achieving the things you want in life. Step up and set all doubts aside; believe that you were born to be an achiever. You will be powerful and able to manifest all the things you want and desire.

Activate the power of belief that lies dormant inside you. Use it to make your goals and dreams a reality. It's your choice; it always was, and it always will be. So, go ahead and choose success in all the things you endeavor.

Powerful Quotes about Belief to Take with You

We can do only what we think we can do.
We can be only what we think we can be.
We can have only what we think we can
have. What we do, what we are, what we
have, all depend upon what we think

—ROBERT COLLIER

The only thing that stands between a man and
what he wants from life is often merely the will to
try it and the faith to believe that it is possible

—RICHARD M. DEVOS

What the mind of man can conceive and
believe, the mind of man can achieve.

—NAPOLEON HILL

I found that I could find the energy...that
I could find the determination to keep on
going. I learned that your mind can amaze
your body, if you just keep telling yourself,
I can do it, I can do it, and I can do it

—JOHN ERICKSON

The mind is the limit. As long as the mind can
envision the fact that you can do something, you
can do it, as long as you really believe 100 percent.

—ARNOLD SCHWARZENEGGER

In order to succeed we must
first believe that we can.

—MICHAEL KORDA

BELIEF AFFIRMATIONS

- MY BELIEFS ARE IN HARMONY WITH MY GOALS.
- I KNOW ANYTHING IS POSSIBLE, THROUGH MY EMPOWERING BELIEFS.
- I CREATE PERFECT BELIEF IN MY ABILITY. TO SUCCEED BY REPETING MY DESIRES.
- I EDIT AND IMPROVE MY BELIEFS, DAILY.
- I EVOLVE MY BELIEFS FOR MY OWN BETTERMENT, DAILY.
- I EXAMINE MY PAST BELIEFS AND RELEASE THOSE WHICH NO LONGER SERVE ME.
- I LET MY THINKING EXCEED MY EXISTING BELIEFS, DAILY.
- I RELEASE PAST LIMITING BELIEFS AND PRACTICE POSITIVE NEW ONES, DAILY.
- I REPLACE PAST LIMITING BELIEFS WITH NEW EMPOWERING ONES, DAILY.
- MY CURRENT CIRCUMSTANCES ARE MIRRORS THAT INDICATE MY BELIEFS.
- WHATEVER I BELIEVE ABOUT MYSELF IS WHAT I BECOME.
- WHO I AM REFLECTS WHAT I BELIEVE.
- MY BELIEFS EMPOWER ME TO MANIFEST THE THINGS I DESIRE.

COURAGE

Courage is a special kind of knowledge; the knowledge of how to fear what ought to be feared, and how not to fear what ought not to be feared. From this knowledge comes an inner strength that subconsciously inspires us to push on in the face of great difficulty. What can seem impossible is often possible, with courage.

—Motivational Quotes

Courage

———⟨≈⟩———

COURAGE IS THE MENTAL OR moral strength to venture, persevere, and withstand danger, fear, or difficulty. When I think about courage, the one thing that comes to mind is all the brave soldiers throughout history who have given their lives in the line of duty. I'm a veteran, and I was called to duty during the Operation Desert Storm conflict.

"In August 1990, the army of the dictator Saddam Hussein of Iraq attacked and captured the neighboring country of Kuwait, setting off an international crisis in the Middle East. It was feared that Hussein might next attack Saudi Arabia, seizing the oil supplies on which much of the world depends. The United Nations gathered allied military forces to drive Hussein's army out of Kuwait. Most of these forces were American, but there were also troops from England, France, Saudi Arabia, and some other countries. In January 1991, Operation Desert Storm under the command of "US general" Norman H. Schwarzkopf was unleashed. Allied planes pounded the Iraqi army with bombs and missiles. The air attacks went on for a month, causing great damage. Then, on February 24, allied ground forces moved into Kuwait, smashing through the main Iraqi defenses. At the same time, a powerful force of US Army tanks made a sweeping "left hook" through desert sands to come in behind the Iraqi army. In four days Hussein's army collapsed. Almost all its equipment was destroyed, and 175,000 Iraqi soldiers surrendered. Operation Desert Storm was a spectacular victory, and Kuwait was liberated. To all the brave courageous men and women of the armed forces, I salute you. My deployment to Operation Desert Storm taught me a valuable lesson about courage. Being fearful in time of adversity is a normal and natural occurrence. The key is to fill the fear but do it anyway. This is how you build courage and confidence. Don't let fear interfere with your ability to perform.

Before you finish this chapter, you will learn ways in which you can become more courageous. **Courage is the ability to do something that requires you to come out of your comfort zone.** What have you been thinking about doing? Is it because of fear that you haven't taken any action yet? What I want you to realize is that you can develop the courage you need to go after your dreams.

Just like how a journey of a thousand miles begins with a single step, your journey to develop courage can also start small. I do believe that you can take that small step. What I don't want you to do is to think too much about what other people are going to say. Don't allow what other people think stop you, it is your dream that is not going to be realized. You may be wondering what that has to do with courage. Everything! Because it's courage that you need to act on your dreams despite what other people think of you or of the dream that you are pursuing.

Courage is not about finding the easiest way out. In all honesty, it is not always easy, but, as you may have already heard, nothing worth having comes easy. It's important to have courage because it helps you to do things others sometimes only think about. If you are ever going to live your best life, you are going to need courage. Maya Angelou summed it up perfectly: "Courage is the most important of all the virtues because without courage, you can't practice any other virtues consistently." If you think about it, you'll realize that this is true.

Before going any further, I want to ask you another important question. What is the mind-set of the people you spend the most time with? "What does that have to do with courage?" you might ask. I'm glad you did. People who are negative, pessimistic, and doubtful will make you think you don't have it in you to do the things you want to do. Therefore, you may end up not developing the courage to ever act on your dreams. The people you want to be around when you want to do something worthwhile with your life are the people who are positive, focused, and living with purpose.

Throughout your life you will encounter situations and circumstances that may require you to demonstrate courage.

Adolescents and young adults are often faced with decisions that require courage. Saying no to friends who offer them alcohol or drugs or standing up to bullies are ways to engage courage.

When people challenge themselves to do something that up till now they were not capable of doing, they acquire courage. When courage is actively engaged, it acts as a great self-esteem and confidence booster. **Each time you stand up, speak up, and face your fears with courage, you build self-confidence and self-esteem for lifetime.** Feel the fear, but do it anyway. When you exude confidence, it shows. When you don't exhibit courage in times of fear, it can confine you psychologically to disbelief, self–doubt, and inhibition.

You will never know where or when you may have to show courage. The key is to be prepared to use it in any situation. If you want to be courageous, practice courage until it is a part of your disposition. Then courage will become an unconscious habit in your daily undertaking, just like getting up, taking a shower, putting your clothes on, brushing your teeth, and going to work.

Courage is a way of life, so make it part of your routine. Before you can acquire any habit or character trait, you must have a strong desire or willingness to do so. Contemplating the alternative, which would be to live in fear or a position of great vulnerability, should provide ample motivation.

Reading about the courageous acts of others can inspires us and offers examples for all of us. You can find lessons of courage in everyday life and throughout the annals of history. You can read stories of courageous people and let these stories inspire you to be courageous when you are faced with fear and adversity.

Take into consideration the Good Samaritans who step in to keep a victim from being robbed or molested, or even give their lives to save someone else. Look at the brave men and women of the armed forces who give their lives on the battlefield, so we can enjoy freedom.

Policemen display courage every day as they fight against crime and criminals to keep civilians safe. Firefighters show courage when they go out to fight raging fires and save victims in the face of devastation. Courage is displayed in entertainment, sports, and businesses as well.

There are many places where you can find people displaying courage. As you know, courage is important to achieve your dreams. Watch people who display courage to inspire you to do the same. Despite what you are going through or where you are on your journey in life, bear in mind you too can develop courage.

Muster the strength to activate the power of your courage in time of fear. If you want to activate courage you can start by exposing yourself to what you fear. By facing your fear, the fear will disappear. It is important that you practice it daily. I personally had a phobia of heights until I learn how to parachute, after jumping from a plane several times my fear of heights has dissipated tremendously.

I must let you know, though: just like any other habits or character traits, courage can take time to develop. So, when you start on the journey of activating courage in your life you need to be patient with yourself. You will see the results if you persevere.

It is going to take courage to speak up. It is going to take courage to voice your opinion. It is going to take courage to go after your dream. Whether you are an employee, a student, or an entrepreneur, you have things you want to share that can benefit others. If you keep it to yourself, you'll never know. If you are not yet comfortable with sharing with people you are not close with, you can share your ideas and dreams with a trusted friend.

Remember, to overcome your fear you must expose yourself to what you fear. That could be sharing your ideas with your boss, who could give you a promotion or share your problem-solving idea with the world. Have the courage to speak your mind during those conversations where others present conflicting views. So many people develop antisocial and shy personality traits because they are afraid to speak what they are thinking. Speak your mind, and it will clear your consciousness.

Don't allow unwanted thoughts to build up in your subconscious mind. These thoughts can be unpleasant and cause pressure to build up, which will lead to hypertension. Your conscious mind is like a universe, constantly expanding. Free your consciousness by speaking your mind. Conflicting opinions can be unpleasant, but not speaking your mind can lead to much worse unpleasantness.

Do you have the courage to stand up for what you believe in? Take courage to stand up for what you believe. As we discussed in the first chapter, your beliefs are an intricate part of your lifestyle, the foundation for how you view the world that you live in. Our beliefs govern how we act in society. Take the courage to stand up for what right and just, also to follow laws, rules, and regulations. Have the courage to execute discipline and self-control when you feel society is not fair and just. Standing up doesn't mean acting out: learn to control your emotions. Mark Twain has said, "Courage is not absence of fear. It is acting despite it."

The sign of a courageous person then is someone who feels fear, recognizes that fear, and still goes on to do what he or she believes is right. Feel the fear, and do it anyway. The process of developing courage is doing what you fear repeatedly until the fear dissipates. Fear is only a word associated with a predetermined condition. Fear can only affect you if you allow it to. **Don't let fear control you—you control it.** You are equipped with the power to overcome any self-defeating thought patterns.

You are a brave knight, riding out to face life head-on and fighting everyday challenges. Courage is what you show on your journey when you face challenge and conflict with strength. It is stronger than fear. It can survive anything. Although you might falter and stumble, courage is what picks you up again, dusts you off, and sets you persistently on your path to make a difference and to be the best person that you can possibly be. Courage is the energy of the truth in your heart. Be guided by courage. It is your companion on your journey to overcome and conquer fear or whatever you decide to undertake.

Courage is not a quality you are or aren't born with. Courage is a quality characteristic trait that may or may not have been passed down to you from the genes of your parents. If the quality trait of courage is not a part of your disposition or is not an innate part of you, take the necessary steps to gain it. It's one that can be acquired, honed, and cultivated. Every day normal people summon the courage to overcome and conquer both physical and psychological barriers to accomplish their goals and objectives.

Courage is the mental and emotional awareness and ability to deal with difficult, challenging, and seemingly impossible circumstances. It is the ability to confront fear, pain, danger, uncertainty, intimidation, and other threats.

When you develop courage, you arm yourself with the power and skill to confront problems and deal with adversity head-on. It's a psychological muscle that helps us deal with life's challenges. Why do you develop character muscles? You do so because it strengthens you and helps you build resistance and resilience to adversity. Today so many people resort to various harmful and counterproductive substances to deal with problems; a healthy supply of courage is without a doubt the wiser alternative. Courage is the remedy you need to deal with problems, take responsibility for your life, and reach for your aspirations.

Commit to develop courage. It is a trait that will help you build additional strength to live a productive, happy, and meaningful life. It is yet another step toward taking responsibility for your state of mind, your circumstances, and your well-being.

As Maxwell Maltz points out: "We must have courage to bet on our ideas, to take the calculated risk, and to act. Everyday living requires courage if life is to be effective and bring happiness".

Sometimes the most courageous people experience fear and trepidation; John Wayne said, "Courage is being scared to death and saddling up anyway." Ask any soldier or warrior who had to venture forth in battle. Few would deny feeling fear and uncertainty beforehand.

Before you can acquire any habit or character trait, you must have a strong desire or willingness to do so. Contemplating the reward and benefit for making such a positive change in your life.

You can start by doing small things to help you overcome the fear of stepping out of your comfort zone. On your road to becoming a more courageous person, start with the little thing in your life. Go to that next social gathering with friends and get acquainted. Ask that cute girl or guy out on a date. Sure, it may be scary, but feel the fear and do it anyway. If you normally hold back and are afraid to speak up at work, offer your opinion and suggestions at the next office meeting. Slowly, build up your courage by doing the things you would typically shy away from. Building courage in this way can help you when it's time to quit that job you are not suited for or leave a relationship that you've long since outgrown.

A large part of developing courage is having faith in your own abilities, faith in a higher power, and faith that things will work out. This type of confidence comes from maintaining positive attitude and visualizing a favorable outcome. A courageous mind-set is the product of faith, self-confidence, and positive thinking. You gain experience, confidence, and strength each time you step out, face your fears, and do the things you think you can't do. You have everything to gain and nothing to lose.

Courage is what counts, and if you lose it you lose everything. Start a new chapter in your life centered on being more courageous in the things you pursue and undertake. This includes goals, dreams, aspirations, successes, and happiness. It doesn't matter the length of your lifespan.

A life of one hundred years can be a tragedy if you don't overcome and conquer your fears. If you learn to conquer your fears, the life of one day can be triumphant. You will always experience feelings of fear and anxiety whenever you try something new. Failure is not fatal, and learning is a process. The greatest wars are fought within the self. You are your worst enemy or biggest hero. Life is a test of your willpower.

Ann Landers couldn't have said it better: "If I were asked to give what I consider the single most useful bit of advice for all humanity it would be this: Expect trouble as an inevitable part of life and when it comes, hold your head high, look it square in the eye and say, 'I will be bigger than you. You cannot defeat me.'"

Powerful Quotes about Courage to Take With you

You gain strength, courage and confidence
by every experience which you must stop
and look fear in the face. You must do
the thing you think you cannot do

—ELEANOR ROOSEVELT

Courage is doing what you're afraid to do.
There can be no courage unless you're scared

—EDDIE RICKENBACKER

He who loses wealth loses much; he who loses a
friend loses more; but he that loses courage loses all

—CERVANTES

Success is never final, and failure is never
fatal; it's courage that counts

—UNKNOWN

Courage is the capacity to confront
what can be imagined

—**Leo Rosten**

Obstacles will look large or small to you
according to whether you are large or small

—**Orison Swett Marden**

COURAGE AFFIRMATIONS

- I AM COURAGEOUS.
- I AM BRAVE.
- I AM FEARLESS.
- I STAND UP FOR MYSELF.
- I AM DEVELOPING COURAGE.
- I CAN HANDLE ANYTHING THAT COME MY WAY.
- I AM STRONG AND WORTHY OF COURAGE.
- I FACE MY FEAR AND DO IT ANYWAY.
- I AM COURAGEOUS WHEN OTHERS ARE SCARED.
- MY COURAGE HELPS TO INSPIRE OTHERS.
- I AM STRONG AND WORTHY.
- I COMMIT TO DEVELOP COURAGE IN MY LIFE.

DESIRE

Desire alone is not enough. But to lack desire, means to lack a key ingredient to success. Many a talented individual failed because they lacked desire. Many victories have been snatched by the underdog because they wanted it more. So, if you desire intensely and you act upon it, then everything stands within your reach.

—MOTIVATIONAL QUOTES

Desire

———⊱∽⊰———

THE WORLD OF BOXING HAS turnout some great boxer, but none of them will be more popular than the great Muhammad Ali:

"During the 1960's and 1970's, no person in American sports was more famous than world heavyweight boxing champion Muhammad Ali. Ali's fame resulted from more than just his boxing title. He was an outspoken supporter of civil rights, and a role model for young African-Americans. He also had a noteworthy personality and a gift for creating amusing poems. Born Cassius Marcellus Clay, Jr., in 1942, he first came to world attention in 1960 when he won the light-heavy-weight Olympic boxing championship. Following this amateur victory, he turned professional and in 1964 took the heavyweight title away from Sonny Liston. In a rematch, Liston went down in the first round for another Ali victory. The boxing authorities took Ali's title away in 1967 when he refused military service in the Vietnam War for religious reasons; the US Supreme Court reversed this decision in 1971. Ali went on to defeat George Foreman in 1974 and regain the championship. In 1978, he lost to Leon Spinks, but then defeated him the same year, thus becoming the only boxer to win the title three times. Ali retired in 1981 with a remarkable record of Fifty-five wins and just five losses".

Napoleon Hill was correct: the starting point of all achievement is desire. Understanding desire and learning how to use it to benefit your need to succeed are two different things. To better understand desire, let's get a clear definition of desire.

Desire is a strong feeling of wanting to have something or wishing for something to happen. It is an attraction toward something, whether it's a material object, a situation, or a circumstance. For example, some people have the natural desire to help others. That desire helps them to stay motivated and find means of carrying out what they want to accomplish.

Desire is important to discuss because it's one of the main ingredients in achieving success. In fact, it is also tied to our ability to become more successful and productive citizens. It is a success characteristic you can use to help achieve your goals, dreams, and aspirations in life. In the pyramid of success, desire is used with belief, imagination, and goals to lay a strong foundation that will help you succeed. The objective of your desire in this case would be to achieve the goals, dreams, and aspirations that you believe will benefit you personally and professionally.

Desire is the need to achieve more than the ordinary. It's the magnetic attraction toward something we would like to have. The urge to possess something can range from weak to strong. The stronger the desire, the more apt you'll be to act.

Desire is one of the characteristics of successful people. The strong desire for what you want to achieve is what's going to help you to meet the challenges of life and in turn give you the strength to push through when things don't go as planned. That means making the sacrifice will be easier because you know the payoff will be well worth the effort. Focus on what is vitally important, and don't be side-tracked by what doesn't matter. We are constantly bombarded with images that create the impulse for desire. This is an ongoing process you should learn to deal with as your life's journey unfolds.

Fulfilling your desires can become an addiction. Accomplishing our desires can bring great satisfaction; it's all relevant to seeking our goals and dreams.

Desire is a driving force triggered through visualization and imagination. What you see has a greater impact on your subconscious mind, greater than the other senses' effects. Products are developed and advertised to entice our desire to possess them. This is done by subliminal messages and hypnosis. The more you want to possess an item, the more desire is aroused within us. Once you accomplish or acquire the thing you desire, the mind will quickly move to the next desire.

When we go shopping for groceries and clothes, our desire increases when we see things that are visually appealing. If we can't acquire what we want immediately, the thought will remain in our subconscious mind, increasing the urge and need to possess it. Desire is basic to being human, and society programs us to desire what we see. Proper management of desires requires an awareness of desires. To transcend desires, learn how to cultivate the right desires.

Focus on the desires that directly relate to the issue at hand; your need to achieve success by attaining your goals, dreams, and aspirations. It is important to recognize the value and worth of desire. Develop a strategy to recognize quality characteristics of desire and use it to acquire the objects of your desire that help you become more successful in life. Properly managed and focus desire is a common denominator for building a sound foundation to achieve success.

I don't know what you want to achieve in life, but one thing that I do know is that just wishing for what you want is not going to make it happen. Wishing is not compelling. It is the desire for what you want that's going to compel you to act. Remember, desire is the starting point for all achievement.

Therefore, if you wish to achieve a goal, that goal needs to be backed by desire. Right now, you may be thinking to yourself, "How can I cultivate the burning desire to achieve the things I want?" By the way, desire is what is going to help you keep going even when you are tempted to quit. So, here are some ways that you can cultivate your own desire.

If you know what you would like to accomplish, you can place images of the things you desire, visible in your immediate environment to stimulate your mind daily. The more you see or think about what you want, the stronger the desire gets for what you want. You can also cultivate the desire for what you want to achieve by surrounding yourself with like-minded people.

When you are around people who constantly reflect the same mind-set, or talk about achieving the things you desire, it helps you to stay focused on what you want to achieve in life. Therefore, the company of like-minded people not only helps to cultivate your desire but also helps you to maintain your desire for what you want to achieve.

We formulate images with our mind, and we cultivate desires for those images using our imagination. Then we attempt to realize those desires. The dynamic forces of desire have influenced you throughout your life even before your age of enlightenment. Desire has been preprogrammed into your subconscious mind through your senses. This makes desire a simple form of physical pleasure. Desire is extremely powerful because it's the urge that compels people to attain the things they desire in life. Positive desire is what you want to keep you inspired and motivated. This will keep you striving to achieve your goals, dreams, and aspirations.

Your beliefs and imagination are the sources that fuel desire; without them desire wouldn't exist. From the perspective of personal development, I would like to address this from a whole perspective: mind, body, and spirit. When the mind desires food we read, when the body desires food we eat, and when the spirit desires food we meditate and pray. They are separate entities that require different sources to fulfill their needs.

The dynamics of desire can arise from many probable sources. These are the goals, dreams, and aspirations you visualize and imagine and try to manifest or bring to fruition. They can be personal, spiritual, or physical; your desires might be related to career, business, finances, wealth, health, fitness, recreation, entertainment, family, friends, relationships, and so on.

Desire is the force that drives you to act to attain the things that bring you closer to living a lifestyle of abundance and happiness. What you visualize and imagine will generate the inner thought activities that will in turn strengthen your desire. When you have a strong desire for something, you normally do whatever it takes to have it, even if that means you take a little risk to see your desire through. This isn't a bad thing because you were born dynamic, continually evolving and changing. The strategies in this book will help you manifest your desire and make them a reality. Remember, happiness depends on your ability to manifest the things you desire in life.

Desire is a key characteristic for achieving what you want to experience in life; it will keep you motivated and inspired

to keep reaching and striving for success. When you have a burning desire for the things you want, you become unstoppable. It can channel your thoughts and imagination to a future time when your desire will be fulfilled.

Desire can be your best friend or worst enemy depending on how you use it. Most of the objects of your desire relate to materialism, but don't let this contradict the belief system you adhere to. It's going to be up to you not to allow old beliefs to stand in the way of what you desire to have in your life.

Remember, you don't want to have contradicting thoughts about the things you desire. Contradicting thoughts will make it harder to love what you want to experience and manifest in your life. These thoughts can be simple as doubting your own abilities. It's important that you're disciplined in your thinking. Learn how to execute discipline and self-control to prioritize and separate objects of fantasy from what you need. What you need for survival should always take precedent over the things in life you fantasize about. You can use what you desire to stay motivated and inspired to reach things of value in your life.

Learning more about desire should be a specific goal for you. Use it to benefit your existence in this world. Having desires or a burning desire is not only found in a few people; it's in you too, and all you need to do is cultivate it. To start the process of cultivating your burning desire for what you want, shift your immediate environment around to match your desire. Do you want to travel? Do you want to live in a big house? Do you want to graduate? After thinking about what you desire, start putting images of those things in your immediate environment.

Another great way to cultivate your desire for the things you want to experience in your life is to surround yourself with the right people, positive people to be exact. You want to be around people who are going to encourage you. And it's always good to fill your mind with empowering information.

Doing this will help you cultivate the desire to be more, do more, and have more in your life. Use it as a focus to keep you striving for the achievement of your goals and dreams for success. Let your desire for success and happiness in life fuel your existence. It is a useful source to help guide your energy, which will carry you toward fulfillment in every area of your life.

Learn to accept desire because it is a part of life and the world that we live in. Identify with your desires and let go of unwanted thoughts that abate your time and energy. When you weed out the unwanted thoughts, you can utilize that time to enhance the quality desires that will help create balance in all areas of your life. Take responsibility for and control of the content of your desire. It is the opportunity to take direct control of your future. Allocate all resources toward techniques that can help you define the quality of desire that will move you closer to achieving success in life.

Powerful Quotes about Desire to Take with You

Through some strange and powerful principle of "mental chemistry" which she has never divulged, nature wraps up in the impulse of strong desire, "that something" which recognizes no such word as "impossible," and accepts no such reality as failure.

—**NAPOLEON HILL**

The greatest trouble with most of us is that our demands upon ourselves are so feeble, the call upon the great within of us so weak and intermittent that it makes no impression upon the creative energies; it lacks the force that transmutes desires into realities.

—**ORISON SWETT MARDEN**

Nothing stops the man who desires to achieve. Every obstacle is simply a course to develop his achievement muscle. It's a strengthening of his powers of accomplishment.

—**ERIC BUTTERWORTH**

You can have anything you want if you want it badly enough. You can be anything you want to be, have anything you desire, accomplish anything you set out to accomplish if you will hold to that desire with singleness of purpose.

—ROBERT COLLIER

All our dreams can come true if we have the courage to pursue them.

—WALT DISNEY

DESIRE AFFIRMATIONS

- I AM CONFIDENT THROUGH MY DESIRES.
- EVERYDAY I MOVE ONE STEP CLOSER TO EVERYTHING I WANT.
- MY DESIRES FLOWS TO ME NOW AND I AM FILLED WITH GRATITUDE.
- WHAT I SEEK IS ALREADY WITHIN ME.
- I TAKE PERSONAL ACTION TO REALIZE MY DREAMS AND DESIRES.
- I MANIFEST MY DESIRES IN A TIMELY AND EFFECTIVE WAY.
- I AM MAGNETIC TO MY OWN DESIRES.
- INTUITIVE ANSWERS COME TO ME THROUGH MY DESIRES.
- I FOLLOW MY HEARTS TRUE DESIRES.
- I ATTRACT ALL THAT I DESIRE HERE AND NOW.
- WHAT I DESIRE IN RETURN DESIRES ME.
- ALL THAT I DESIRE WILL COME TO PASS.

EXCELLENCE

———✸———

Going far beyond the call of duty, doing more than others expect, this is what excellence is all about. And it comes from striving, maintaining the highest standards, looking after the smallest detail, and going the extra mile. Excellence means doing your very best, in everything, in every way.

—MOTIVATIONAL QUOTES

MASTER STRATEGY IV
Excellence

———oeeo———

SOME TIME AGO, A FRIEND of mind sent this story to me, and I want to share it with you.

A German once visited a temple under construction where he saw a sculptor making an idol of God. Suddenly he noticed a similar idol lying nearby. Surprised, he asked the sculptor, "Do you need two statues of the same idol?"

"No," said the sculptor without looking up, "we need only one, but the first one got damaged at the last stage."

The gentlemen examined the idol and found no apparent damage. "Where is the damage?" he asked.

"There is a scratch on the nose of the idol," said the sculptor, still busy with his work.

"Where are you going to install the idol?"

The sculptor replied that it would be installed on a pillar twenty feet high. "If the idol is that far, who is going to know that there is a scratch on the nose?" the gentlemen asked.

The sculptor stopped his work, looked up at the gentlemen, smiled and said, "I will know it."

Excellence is the quality of being outstanding or extremely good. You don't strive for excellence to satisfy other people; you strive for excellence for your own satisfaction, for excellence is a drive that comes from within. Excellence is just below perfection, so this means that you have taken your level of performance to an extremely high level. When you strive for excellence, you are setting the bar high for yourself. This is great because you are willing to challenge your ability to reach for the next level.

Most people are satisfied where they are, afraid to even make a conscious effort to try to push through or go to the next level. Because of striving for excellence, you may unveil hidden potential you never knew you had. Your success in life will sometimes require that you search for the absolute best you have to offer. Life is here for you to challenge it, to do more than the minimum or ordinary.

So, go ahead: strive for excellence and find your fullest potential. In pursuit of going to their first-ever Super Bowl, Vincent Lombardi told his team, the Green Bay Packers, "We will strive for perfection and in the process, we will find excellence."

I believe everyone has the potential for excellence. Do you believe you can be excellent? You must dig deep within to pull it out. You should reach for perfection knowing you may not attain it, but if you gain excellence, you have accomplished a lot. Some people have the innate drive and determination to be successful. Others must be motivated and inspired to challenge themselves and develop their own ability to succeed. Excellence is a key characteristic that will set you on a pinnacle high above the average.

Excellence is a philosophy. If you want to be excellent, you must research and define what excellence is. Learn more about it and incorporate it into your lifestyle. You can look in any career or profession and find ordinary people doing extraordinary things that make them stand out from the rest. Let these people be a model for you. Emulate what they do. Take your game to the next level. Don't limit yourself; push yourself.

Today we have a variety of resources that can help us transcend mediocrity. There are mentors, coaches, and counselors in all professional fields. These professionals reside in high schools, colleges, and the corporate sector. Their goal and objective are to help people realize their full potential. Don't be afraid to reach out. Allocate your resources and take advantages of these services. They will only make you better. Your greatness is waiting for you. If you don't believe me try leaving your comfort zone.

On your road to good fortune and abundance there will be ebb and flow. Don't give up. Keep your eyes on the prize. During your highs ride the wave; stay motivated and inspired. Take your lows with a grain of salt, and don't let them deter your journey; keep moving forward.

Stay current by continually improving all aspects of your character. This is a part of demanding excellence from who you are. Human growth and development requires change. Change is inevitable. If you don't improve as you grow and develop, you will become stagnant. When you allow yourself to stagnate, you abate the ability to evolve. Your journey to excellence can be long and difficult, but you have it in you to be extraordinary.

Recognize that each success can be a stepping-stone to excellence. Celebrate the small wins. You may demand excellence, but are you willing to sacrifice to experience what it mean to be excellent? The prize is worth a hundred times the sacrifice. The measure of your success will be determined by your ability to recognize the important of striving for excellence in all your endeavors. Excellence is what lets you stand out from the rest. Excellence is what comes when you put your best foot forward every day despite life's trials.

You may have heard the cliché "Practice makes perfect." It's not just a cliché: practice really does make perfect. You must be willing to practice until you reach a level of excellence. Excellence is something that you continuously practice. When you become excellent, your ability to perform without making marginal errors or mistake increases by 99.9 percent. You can also use the power of creative mental images to practice. It has been proven that people who use their mind as a source of practicing increase their performance ability by 50 percent. People who demand excellence practice daily. It is a process of becoming one with success by totally immersing or becoming one with what you desire.

There is a right way to practice and a wrong way to practice. Practicing daily has its advantages. Make sure you follow the initial instructions and practice the right way. If you practice the wrong way, you're practicing will be in vain.

Make a conscious effort to learn the proper way to do anything you undertake. Allocate resources and solicit help from professionals who are willing to train you correctly. Use recording devices to help identify strengths, weaknesses, and mistakes. This can apply to sports activities, entertainment, learning a new language or giving speeches.

Remember, failure is natural part of the process when you are striving for success or trying to attain excellence. Don't let failure get you down. Do it again and again and again until you get it right. Keep a positive mental attitude. Attitude is everything as you reach for success. Demand excellence by being consistent when you practice.

Identify your strengths and weaknesses, seeking to improve both aspects. Working on your strengths can only make them greater, and working on your weaknesses will make them better. You double your improvement. Analyze what you do daily by keeping a written journal. Some days you may want to focus more attention on your weakest points. Identify what needs to be improved and make the necessary correction. Learn how to work on the whole aspect of improving your ability. This will increase your overall ability to perform at any level.

What is the force that is driving you to be excellent? You must have a burning desire that motivates and inspires you to reach for excellence. If you are seeking excellence for your own self-gratification, this is a good reason. Most people are driven by some external force such as money, power, fame, and so on. Don't get me wrong; there's nothing wrong with using external stimuli to motivate you to do better.

However, chances are, when things get difficult you will be more apt to abort this externally motivated desire to achieve excellence. When it's personal, your chances of persevering increase greatly because you'll feel more inspired when times are difficult. If you want to be your absolute best, strive for excellence.

Excellence is a key quality characteristic that is paramount when it comes to achievement. Excellence is easy to measure: It's the distance between mediocrity and superiority. All successful people go far and beyond to attain a certain level of achievement. They are willing to sacrifice to separate themselves from the rest and create distance between their work and the average standard of achievement. What are you prepared to do? Will you challenge yourself to explore beyond your current capabilities? You can be excellent in the things you endeavor.

The corporate sector absolutely cherishes employees who are stellar in their ability to perform work tasks. These employees are recognized and respected for the excellence they exhibit. In the world of entertainment, you see actors and actress recognized for their stellar performances at the Oscars, Academy Awards, the People's Choice Awards, and others.

These awards are established to recognize the people who perform at a level of excellence. In the world of sports, championships are won because of excellence, and players are compensated for their ability to perform at a higher standard. Those players who perform on an excellent level receive higher pay and compensation.

As you can see, excellence has its proper place in society. It's worth all the effort, time, and sacrifice you put in to achieve it. You hold the key to your success: take your game of achievement to the next level by doing more than expected. If you go beyond and develop your abilities and talents, in the process learn how to use the whole of those talents.

You will experience a satisfaction few people will ever have the opportunity to experience. The greatest gift you can give yourself is the ability to create and develop the talents that lie dormant within you. Take your talents to the next level by striving for excellence. If you truly want to do more, be more, and have more, it's solely up to you; it's your choice.

Powerful Quotes about Excellence to Take with You

There is an infinite difference between a little wrong and just right, between fairly good and the best, between mediocrity and superiority.

—**ORISON SWETT MARDEN**

Success has always been easy to measure. It is the distance between one's origins and one's final achievement.

—**MICHAEL KORDA**

When a man has done his best, has given his all, and in the process supplied the needs of his family and his society, that man has succeeded.

—**MACK DOUGLAS**

The quality of person's life is in direct
proportion to their commitment to excellence,
regardless of their chosen field of endeavor.

—**Vincent T. Lombardi**

If a man has a talent and cannot use it, he has
failed. If he has a talent and uses only half of
it, he has partly failed. If he has a talent and
learns somehow to use the whole of it, he has
gloriously succeeded, and won a satisfaction
and a triumph few men ever know.

—**Thomas Wolfe**

EXCELLENCE AFFIRMATIONS

* MY EXCELLENCE IS INCREASINGLY IN ALL THAT I THINK, SAY AND DO!
* I OPERATE PRECISELY AND SMOOTHLY, RESULTING IN EXCELLENT PERFORMANCE AND SPECIFIC, MEASURABLE RESULTS.
* I AM ORDERLY, ORGANIZED AND EFFECTIVE, THROUGH EXCELLENCES.
* I EXCEL IN EVERYTHING I SET OUT TO DO.
* I DEMOSTRATE EXCELLENCE DAILY.
* I THIRST FOR KNOWLEDGE AND STRIVE FOR EXCELLENCE.
* I STRIVE TO BE AN EXCELLENT PERSON IN LIFE.
* I FOCUS MY MIND ON ABSOLUTE EXCELLENCE.
* THE ENERGY OF EXCELLENCE IS INFUSED INTO ALL MY LIFE'S ACTIVITIES.
* I FOCUS MY ATTENTION ON ACHIEVING A HIGH LEVEL OF PERFORMANCE.
* I AM COMMITTED TO ACHIEVING EXCELLENCE.
* I AM A PERSON OF EXCELLENCE.

FAILURE

---

*Successful people are not afraid to fail. They
have the ability to accept their failures and
continue on, knowing that failure is a natural
consequence of trying. The law of failure is one of
the most powerful of all the success laws because
you only really fail when you quit trying.*

—Motivational Quotes

MASTER STRATEGY V
Failure

—⟨∞⟩—

THE FAMOUS QUOTE "TO ERR is human" is not quite accurate. This "motivational" statement implies that humanity can be defined by failure. I believe humanity is not defined by failure but rather by the overcoming of it.

Failure is the lack of success. A failure is not achieving the desired end or ends. This definition simply means that a person did not achieve what he had set out to accomplish. It makes no judgment about the person performing the act. Being a person means that you are human like the rest of us. Since people tend to judge your worth based on successes or failures. A mistake or the inability to achieve a certain end does not make you less of a person. It does not define who you are.

You are human being, born to make mistakes. Most people just give up if they don't achieve their desired objective. But you don't have to let failure define who you are. Use the power of your mind to overcome and conquer failure. Use positive affirmations to recondition your mind and defeat failure.

What are you prepared to do to change your mind-set about failure? Consider this: failure is a natural consequence of trying. You need to condition your mind to believe that failing is not the end of the world. It's only a setback that brings you closer to achieving your goals. Failure can only affect you if you allow it to define who you are. Adopt a positive mind-set. Believe you can accomplish whatever you undertake. You can accomplish anything when you tell your mind, "I can do it."

Remember, it took Thomas Edison one thousand experiments to discover the filament for the light bulb. Are you willing to go the distance until you reach your dreams? Some achievements happen instantly, while others take time, so be patient: it will all come to fruition. You can overcome obstacles more easily if you believe and have a positive mental attitude. Remember the shame associated with failure is just an awkward feeling, it will dissipate once you begin the process of achieving what you want by being successful when you try to accomplish something.

Failure refers to the state or condition of not meeting a desirable or intended outcome, and it may be viewed as the opposite of success. However, many have triumphed from experiencing failure. As we said earlier, failure is the natural consequence of trying. You will only stop failing when you stop trying. Failure has no criteria: it's simply a confidence and self-esteem killer. Your belief about failure will determine the measure of control it has over you. Let failure be a motivating factor that brings out the absolute best in you. John Elway lost four Super Bowls before he won two Super Bowls at the end of his career. As you can see, failure can be a stepping-stone on your path to success. Don't give up because you fail once or twice; that doesn't mean you will continue to fail the rest of your life. I found the following companies and people to be great examples of success overcoming failure:

When Coca Cola started they only sold 400 cokes in the first year. That could have discouraged them. Bill Gates and partner Paul Allen started the Company Traf-O-Data and failed only to start Microsoft and became a multi-billion-dollar success. Dr. Glenn Cunningham, ran the world's fastest mile, in February 1934. New York City's famed Madison Square Garden, this young man who was not expected to survive, who would surely never walk, who could never hope to run, survived a fire accident at his school that devastated the lower half of his body. Bear Grylls survived a parachute accident that partially crushed three of his vertebrae. He would go on to climb Mt. Everest and become a wildlife presenter on the Discovery Channel with, his own show call Man vs Wild. Chris Gardner failed as a salesman only to become the CEO and founder of Christopher Gardner International Holding. His life was portrayed in a Hollywood film called The Pursuit of Happyness', which became a blockbuster. After Twitter and Facebook rejected Brian Action, he teams up with another Yahoo alum and built the cloud-based messaging none as Whatsapp. Facebook acquired Whatsapp in 2014 for about $19 billion USD in cash and stock, making Action's net worth around $3.8 billion. Oprah Winfrey publicly failed several diet attempts before becoming an inspiration for looking great after fifty. If you have tried and didn't succeed keep trying until you do, because you can.

Setbacks, disappointments, rejections, and unsuccessful attempts were not failures to these people. They were steps to their success. That's the difference between people who are winning at success and people who aren't. How you deal with your setbacks (big or small) will determine your results. You see, failure is not the lack of success. Failure is inspiration to motivate you to succeed. Failure is not staying down when you trip or stumble. Don't give up, check out, or shut down. Keep moving; stay your course.

I'm sure everyone can identify with a point in their career when they were fired, passed over for a promotion, failed to get a raise, or couldn't achieve something that was extremely important. Events like these may have affected your confidence or made you feel like a failure. But they don't have to determine your future or stop you from continuing to pursue your career aspirations. Every time you encounter a setback, the key is to get back up dust yourself off, and continue trying.

Throughout your life and career, you will encounter struggles, frustrations, and disappointments. How you view your disappointments, falls, and setbacks will affect your success. Will they be a stepping-stone for your success or a brick wall that hinders your progress?

Ralph Waldo Emerson said, "Men succeed when they realize that their failures are the preparation for their victories." Don't take your falls, setbacks, and disappointments personally; if you do, they will hinder your progress. Let them be stepping-stones to help you win at successfully achieving your goals and dreams.

People who are winning at living a fulfilled lifestyle don't blame others for what's happened to them, and they don't use other people's definitions for success and failure. They use their own. They know it's not failing to miss their mark, change paths, reassess goals, try something new, or adjust direction. To them, true failure happens when they stop trying to achieve their personal best.

Failure is a part of success. In fact, they complement each other. Look at all the successful people throughout history who didn't let failure determine their ability to succeed. Failure played an intricate role in them becoming successful. Every failure is a lesson within itself. Failure can be a correcting mechanism if you see the desired result. When we look at failure from the right perspective, it can help us see the right way more clearly.

What are you prepared to do on your journey to success? You will never know the measure of your success until you program your mind to overcome failure. Failure is the fear you must conquer. Mistakes can be outcomes and results that propel us in the direction of success, so don't let them discourage you.

Fear is the unpleasant emotion you may experience when facing the unknown. Don't allow fear to keep you from succeeding or fulfilling your goals and dreams. The fear of failure can be a part of your belief system. Perceptions are drawn from past experiences. Don't trust these perceptions because they are part of the past, not the present. You experience the present, and what you do now will create your future. Create a future that revolves around accomplishment and success in life.

Your future can be brighter than ever: set your goals, reach for your aspirations, and let go of the past. Stay in the moment; make life what you want it to be. You control your destination right now in the present. You can have the best life ever when you make life what you want it to be. So, release, relax, and let go of your fear of failure. Failure can be a stepping-stone for your success.

Success is waiting for you; do you have the courage to reach out and take hold of it? You are not a failure. Always draw on the positive not the negative. Discard any thoughts from the past that creative unpleasant feelings. Happiness is the natural order of things. Failure is a part of the negative, so you shouldn't spend a considerable amount of your time thinking about it as being relevant to the past or present.

However, everything you experienced in your life span is relevant—how you dealt with those experiences directly shaped your present. Learn from your mistakes and build off your achievements, then let the past go. The only thing that matters now is the present and the future.

Life is one big odyssey of positive and negative experiences. How you deal with these experiences will determine the measure of your success. Don't waste time worrying about failure: its normal too fail sometimes when you are trying to succeed, failure only purpose is to keep you from true happiness. Live your life, dream big, set your goals and aspirations, and reach them. You are the only person standing in your way.

Failure can only be as dominant as you allow it to be. Success and failure are opposite poles of attraction. Failure can only be canceled by success. Don't give failure the oxygen it needs to survive. You give failure direct power to control your life when you refuse to challenge what it presents.

Every time you succeed at something, no matter how small it might be, you tilt the scale in the favor of success. Cancel the fear of failure. Face your challenges head-on, defeat them, and become victorious in life. Watch the face of failure slowly recede into the distance as you, a new knight in shining armor, arise to overcome and conquer the challenges of life.

Let success dominate your life. Know what it feels like to exude confidence in all situations and circumstances. Time will show that you can transcend your past self who felt like a failure to become a hero with a disposition that exemplifies courage every time you call upon it to perform. Time will change your failures into successes. You may not see results overnight; just be patient, and the process will take root and grow. Your efforts will produce results you can see. All things are relative to time. Your quest to overcome and conquer your fear of failure is relative to time as well.

In conclusion, success is a voyage of discovery. Success is finding out what your true talents are. Cultivate and hone these talents and make them work for you. Life doesn't always reveal its true meaning, so don't be quick to judge the whole of life by a few failing moments. The measure of your success can't be judged by the measure of someone else's success.

Success is the pinnacle of happiness; there are many successful people in the world, and most them are happy. You must choose happiness regardless of the present situation or circumstance. Always strive for improvement in all aspects of your life; let your drive to be successful help manifest your happiness. Happiness is doing what you love and loving what you do.

True winners set their goals and dreams and diligently work to achieve them. As a leader, be careful how you define a "failure" and how quickly you make this judgment. Yes, when you feel you've "missed the mark" or failed, you should seriously examine what you did wrong to learn from the experience! But, remember that failure is relative to time. What may appear to be a failure today may have planted the seeds for success later. Secondly, failure is often success when we see it from a different point of view. What we experience or the "result" may be far different than what we immediately see.

This story was sent to me by a friend. Many years ago, a young struggling cartoonist lost his job when he was told by his boss that he couldn't draw and had no talent. He decided to work for himself and find his own clients. After a long period of struggle and failure, he found only one customer! A minister paid him a very small amount of money to draw advertising for his church. The cartoonist was so downtrodden and pathetic the church allowed him to stay in their mouse-infested garage. While he lived there, he drew cartoons that no one wanted, and nicknamed his favorite little mouse who scurried in the garage Mickey.

From apparent failure Walt Disney transcended disappointment and misfortune to become a success. He achieved this by believing in his vision and his mission along with time and a right perspective. So can you!

Powerful Quotes about Failure to Take with You

The successful man will profit from his
mistakes and try again in a different way.

—DALE CARNEGIE

Remember you will not always win. Some days, the
most resourceful individual will taste defeat. But
there is, in this case, always tomorrow, after you
have done your best to achieve success today.

—Maxwell Maltz

No man ever achieved worth-while success who
did not, at one time or other, find himself with at
least one foot hanging well over the brink of failure.

—NAPOLEON HILL

The freedom to fail is vital if you're going to succeed. Most successful men fail time and time again, and it is a measure of their strength that failure merely propels them into some new attempt at success.

—Michael Korda

Don't be afraid to fail. Don't waste energy trying to cover up failure. Learn from your failures and go on to the next challenge. IT'S OK TO FAIL. If you're not failing, you're not growing.

—H. Stanley Judd

FAILURE AFFIRMATIONS

- I AM A FEARLESS PERSON.
- I TAKE ACTION NOW.
- I AM FREE FROM THE FEAR OF FAILURE.
- I LET CONFIDENCE AND DETERMINATION OVER-SHADOW FEAR.
- FEAR WILL NOT STOP ME FROM SUCCEEDING.
- I PERSIST WHEN FACED WITH FEAR.
- I ACCEPT CHALLENGES WITH OPTIMISM, ENTHUSIASM AND CONFIDENCE.
- I EMBRACE FAILURE TO BECOME STRONGER BY IT.
- I AM COMMITTED TO OVERCOME AND CONQUER THE FEAR OF FAILURE.
- I ALWAYS ACT WITHOUT THE HESITATION OF FEAR.
- I PUSH THROUGH THE FEAR OF FAILURE.
- I WILL SUCCEED.

GOALS

The purpose of goals is to focus our attention. The mind will not reach toward achievement until it has clear objectives. The magic begins when we set goals. It is then that the switch is turned on, the current begins to flow, and the power to accomplish becomes a reality.

—MOTIVATIONAL QUOTES

Goals

———∞∞∞———

GOALS ARE SOMETHING THAT YOU are trying to do or achieve. One formula for achievement reads A=I*M, where A = achievement, I = intelligence, and M = motivation. When motivation equals zero, achievement always equals zero, no matter the degree of intelligence. Similarly, for intelligence: if intelligence equals zero, achievement always equals zero. On the other hand, if your intelligence is high and you are motivated, the greater the chance of you achieving your goals.

As millions watched on television, one of the most dramatic moments in human history took place some 235,000 miles away. The hatch of the Apollo 11 lunar module opened. Commander Neil A. Armstrong, dressed in a bulky space suit, slowly climbed down a ladder. Finally, his boot touched the surface of the moon. "That's one small step for a man," he said, "one giant leap for mankind." Four days earlier, on July 16, 1969, a giant Saturn V Rocket, as tall as a 28-story building, had been launched from Cape Kennedy in Florida. Atop the rocket was the Apollo 11 spacecraft carrying three American astronauts: Neil Armstrong, Edwin E. Adkins, Jr., and Michael Collins. The three-stage rocket provided the thrust to propel the spacecraft to the moon. Apollo 11 then took over, using its own engine to go into orbit around the moon. Then on July 20, the Apollo 11's spider-legged lunar module separated from the rest of the spacecraft and carried Armstrong and Aldrin to a flat area on the moon's surface. The landing was smooth. For the first time, humans had landed on the moon. A dream as old as humanity had been achieved.

Now I would like to talk about goals. **Goals are the fuel that keeps the fire of desire burning bright.** You need goals to keep you actively engaged in your pursuit of what you want to achieve. Goals are a crucial step in building a solid foundation for achieving success. Goals and imagination go hand and hand; both require you to visualize ambitions and aspirations. Use the power of your creative imagination and visualize yourself as a professional doctor, lawyer, pilot, musician, journalist, athlete, writer, CEO, or entrepreneur. The list can go on and on.

Goals are the things that you want to accomplish in your lifetime, and they come in all shapes and sizes. Goals will help motivate and inspire you to take the necessary action to attain your dreams and aspirations. What goals do you have? Ask yourself, "What do I want to achieve?" Remember, goals will help you to stay focused. Many people set goals, but they find themselves unable to reach those goals because they can't stay focused. Therefore, you should write your goals down, so you can identify them daily. If you identify your goals daily, they become deeply rooted in your subconscious mind. This way they will become a part of your daily thinking. Life is one big compilation of thoughts and experiences that control your actions. Let your thoughts and experiences help move you closer to achieving your goals and dreams.

One key element to creating a lifestyle of success is to learn to focus your attention on the things that matter in your life, things that will help you move closer to your destiny. Don't allow unwanted thought patterns, ones that don't apply to you, to preoccupy your mind-set. The great motivational speaker Les Brown talks about mind-set maintenance and development, which is the art of programming your mind for success. You can empower yourself just by setting your mind to focus on the things that will bring you closer to succeeding. The bottom line is this: you are choosing to control how you think because doing so will help you to get what you want out of life. This is also a part of the universal law of attraction. By thinking about something, you draw it closer to you.

It is possible to achieve anything you desire. Look around you at all the people who have attained success. Their success was based on the ability to focus only on the things that were related to them becoming great. However, don't measure your success against theirs; learn how to emulate the thing they did to achieve what they wanted in life.

What you may have to do is change your perception, the image and understanding you have about succeeding at the things you want. Remember, being successful begins in the mind. It's important that you become success oriented, and your goals can help with that. Believe that it is possible, and change your mental point of view, the way you think, about success. Let your goals become a positive driving force to help you manifest the things you desire.

What are you prepared to do? Are you willing to sacrifice where you are in life right now to become what you want to be? Sacrifice is important, but some people aren't willing to give up something or leave their comfort zone to change who they are. It's not about changing who you are.

It's about reprogramming or reinventing yourself to get the most out of who you are. Many people's talents and abilities will remain dormant because they aren't willing to sacrifice or challenge their creativity. (The Bible even says to be transformed by the renewing of your mind). Having goals will help renew your mind because they will help you to think differently. What about you: are you renewing your mind-set with goals? Transform who you are and renew how you think daily. The thought transforms your mind; then you will evolve and see changes in your life.

Goals will serve as your driving force and can be short-, mid-, or long-term. It's up to you, however; you can have all three simultaneously. Short-term goals relate to things that tend to be more urgent. Long-term goals are normally aligned with important things. Use your goals to keep you motivated, inspired, and focused.

Let me say this: believing is one thing, but acting is another. For goals you are required to act if you want to achieve them. If you don't achieve them in a timely manner, you can always reset and try again. The road to good fortune and abundance requires your participation. That is, once you start to move toward what you want, what you want will move toward you.

As I said earlier, happiness is the natural order of things. One way to live a more positive, optimistic, and enthusiastic life is to have goals and manifest your dreams. The anticipation for something good in the future will inspire you to reach for your aspirations. Your future is predestined by what you do in the present. The future is yours to shape.

Be your own surrogate. You're the pilot, captain, conductor, and driver; you have the power and control, but you must learn to take charge of your destination by controlling how you think. If you don't take control of your own destination, something or someone else will.

Make sure your goals are achievable. There shouldn't be a lot of pressure to attain your short-term objectives. For example, you might set a direct long-term goal to eliminate all your debt within a ten-year period. Indirectly the process would have you eliminating your least expensive debt first. This could be considered a short-term goal.

Goals are the fuel that will keep you speeding on the fast track to success. Goals will keep you purpose driven. Chart a course for your future by defining your goals. Your other alternative is to let life shape your future by haphazardly dealing with situations and circumstances as they occur. By the way, I don't think you want that to happen. I choose to set goals and strive to manifest them. That way, you choose to have the life you want.

Everyone that sets a goal may not reach it in a timely manner; don't let that stop you from setting your goals. Make sure your goals are attainable and achievable. You can evaluate your progress and make changes as you go. Acting on your goals is very important; think about what will happen if you don't. Act if you want to see results. If your goals are not achieved in a timely manner, don't get discouraged; keep pushing. Go back to the drawing board, brainstorm ideas, and try it again. Just don't give up!

Some people want instant gratification once they set goals. It will happen in due time. You must remain positive that your goals will come to fruition. Stay devoted and committed to achieving your desired results. Remember, it's possible; you may face challenges and obstacles on the road to success. No matter what, you have within you what it takes to be successful.

What are some reasons some people never reach their goals and dreams? Some reasons might be that they thought about their goals but didn't write them down on paper. Or they never sat down and strategized a concrete action plan to help them attain their goals. It's possible that their goals had no measurable point of progress or no specific time frame for completion. Goals require time, effort, dedication, and action; there are no quick or easy resolutions. You must plan to do your part. Look for resources that will give you guidelines and help teach you how to go about the business of achieving goals.

People place a lot of emphasis on goals because goals can help you manifest the things you want in life. Goals can help you achieve success. You must seize the opportunity and make goal setting a part of your lifestyle. There is no big secret to goal achievement; you are the major ingredient to manifesting your goals. You hold the key and have the power to make your life better with goals.

Goal setting is a major component of personal development because it allows people to work toward their own personal objectives regarding finances, career, health, religion, recreation, etc. Some goals may even be specified as private, confidential, or classified. People do set personal goals. Learn how to manage your goals properly to benefit all areas of your lifestyle. Prioritize your goals to help you focus on what you need to improve. Planning and goal setting will provide a clearer vision for your future and keep you motivated.

The measure of belief you have in your ability to reach a personal goal will also affect that achievement. To achieve intricate and complicated goals requires focus, diligence, and effort. The term of the goal will make no difference. Short- and long-term goals collaborate to achieve success. Success in all fields requires kicking excuses and taking responsibility to make sure it happens. Success in reaching your destiny requires emotional maturity and self-control.

Goal setting will play an intricate role in your life. Goals can remind you to take the necessary action to manifest your dreams and bring them to fruition. Goals really can make a difference in your mission to reach success. To make them happen, write your goals down and specify a deadline. Make your goals specific. If they are specific, you can commit them to memory more easily. Make your goals interesting; interesting goals will motivate and inspire you to act. Develop drive and momentum by acting to resolve your goals immediately after you set each one. To get a better understanding of how to use goals, you should start setting goals for yourself today. This will move you closer to achieving success in your life.

I hope you get the big picture or have a clearer objective about goal setting. Take time to set goals in your lifestyle. Goal setting is one of best and easiest ways to achieve the things you want in life. They will keep you focused and set on the fast track to success. So, go ahead and take the first step to get the things you want out of life: set your goals and reach for them.

In conclusion, I'd like to reiterate the purpose for setting goals. The purpose of goals is to focus our attention. Before you can start the process of achievement, you need to set goals. The goals you set will determine what the future has in store for you. Goals will show you a clear pathway to follow until you arrive at your destination. They will chart a course for you to pursue your desires. Believe in yourself wholeheartedly; initiate the courage necessary to motivate and inspire you to reach all your goals. If you fail, don't take it personally. Consult with your mind and brainstorm all ideas. Use your imagination to design a new path to help achieve the goals you set. Remember, every problem is its own solution.

This mean you can solve any problem by analyzing the problem itself. Goals are an opportunity for you to take control of your destiny. They will help you persist in your effort to achieve success and happiness. They will make sure you are going somewhere in life. Take control and responsibility for your existence; learn how to set goals in life. Goals are powerful; they are a key characteristic to the achievement of success wherever you go. Among the Master Strategies, goals are a powerful tool you can use to motivate and inspire you to greatness.

Powerful Quotes about Goals to Take with You

People with goals succeed because
they know where they're going.

—EARL NIGHTINGALE

Goals help you channel your energy into action.

—LES BROWN

The world has the habit of making room
for the man whose words and actions
show that he knows where he is going.

—NAPOLEON HILL

Whatever you can do or dream you can, begin
it. Boldness has genius, power, and magic in it.

—GOETHE

This one step, choosing a goal and
sticking to it, changes everything.

—SCOTT REED

Goals determine what you're going to be.

—JULIUS ERVING

There is no achievement without goals.

—ROBERT J. MCKAIN

GOALS AFFIRMATIONS

* I CLEARLY VISUALIZE THE ACHIEVEMENT OF MY GOALS.
* TODAY I TAKE ACTION TO REACH MY GOALS.
* I RELEASE RESISTANCE THOUGHTS OF ACHIEVING MY GOALS.
* I AM ACHIEVING MY GOALS.
* I KNOW WHERE I AM GOING, AND EVERY STEP WILL BE IN THAT DIRECTION.
* I LIBERATE MYSELF FROM THE DOUBT OF ACHIEVING MY GOALS.
* I GIVE MYSELF PERMISSION TO ACHIEVE MY GOALS.
* I FOCUS MY MIND AND ENERGY ON THE PROCESS OF ACHIEVING MY GOALS.
* I MOVE OVER, UNDER, THROUGH OR AROUND ANY OBSTACLES IN THE WAY OF ACHIEVING MY GOALS.
* MY ACTION WILL ENSURE I REACH MY GOALS.
* I COMMIT TO ACHIEVE MY GOALS.
* MY GOALS WILL LEAD TO SUCCESS.
* ACHIEVING GOALS COMES NATURAL TO ME.

HONESTY

———⁂———

Before us lie two paths, honesty or dishonesty. The ignorant embark on the dishonest path; the wise on the honest. For in helping others, you help yourself; in hurting others, you hurt yourself. Those who remain honest know the truth; character overshadows money, trust rises above fame. And honesty is still the best policy.

—Motivational Quotes

Honesty

———— ❦ ————

HONESTY IS THE QUALITY OF being fair and truthful. It's all about doing the right thing even if no one is watching. In fact, being honest is not something you just do with others; being honest with yourself is just as important. What you must bear in mind is that being honest will not always be received well by everyone you are honest with.

As you may have heard, sometimes the truth hurts. When you are honest, you don't have to try to remember what you said, because what you have said was true in the first place. Honesty is what will make it easier for people to trust you, and trust is what will strengthen your relationships. Integrity, on the other hand, means abiding in and supporting your morals and ethics. Remember, you must live with yourself and whatever you say; you are going to know even if you don't admit it publicly. The bottom line is, "To thy own self be true."

First and foremost, you cannot have a genuine discussion about honesty without looking at yourself first. If you can't be honest with yourself, how can you be honest with other people? Honesty is a catalyst for integrity. This may require a lot of soul searching.

A discussion about honesty can be painful, especially when your customary disposition is anything other than honest. Together, let's look at honesty as a quality characteristic that can be used to gain leverage on your road to success. I truly believe everyone would like to display an honest character under all circumstances.

Honesty and integrity go hand and hand. When people perceive you to be an honest person, they automatically assume you have morals and ethics. We try to support and abide by our moral and ethical beliefs, but life has a funny way of dealing with people in ways that cause them to alter their personalities and attitudes, so they can adjust and adapt to situations as they occur. No one is perfect. All situations are not the same.

You would be extremely naive to believe everyone you meet has an honest disposition. Life can be one big facade; sometimes it shakes the very core of your belief system. Don't let life dictate how you should think, act, or feel about your own existence. Stay strong and hold on to your honesty and integrity. In the end, you'll see that it was well worth it.

Honesty will always carry the core values that represent trustworthiness and integrity. Use the quality characteristic of honesty on your road to good fortune and success.

Honesty will help you keep a clear conscience. When a person lies, cheats, steals, and hurts others to gain success, she should consider the universal law of karma: as you do unto others, it shall be done unto you. Who wants to walk around with a guilt-ridden conscience because you showed no honesty when dealing with other people? When you reach the pinnacle of success in your life, your mind will be free of guilt, and you can help others to help themselves. Honesty is part of practicing good morals, and dishonesty is immoral in a belief system.

Honesty is important because it's a code of conduct. The Bible talks about honesty. People who claim Christianity should display an honest disposition.

If you want to follow in integrity, you must be honest. The customary practice of being dishonest can compromise your belief. Being honest is about becoming God centered and following in his footsteps. An attitude of dishonesty would move you away from God according to the people of the Bible.

You need to focus more on being honest. Learn how to recognize people who display a dishonest character and don't spend a lot of time dealing with them. Don't set yourself up for a big disappointment Your personality and attitude reflect your character. How you act reflects what you believe. Your character represents who you are and will play a big role in your life.

Learn how to practice honesty because people are constantly judging your character. Honesty is one of God's commandments. He wants us to obey his commandment and follow his example. Honesty should be part of our character; let your character mirror what you believe.

It is not easy to live a lifestyle centered on honesty, but we shouldn't let that make being honest optional. Choosing to have an honest attitude helps you to be more trustworthy. Sometimes it seems that our society favors dishonesty and hypocrisy. Maintain your honesty wherever you go in life. Treat people the way you would want to be treated. Honesty is truly the best policy. Therefore, it's at the top of the success pyramid, remember foundation, formation and leverage. It is for creating leverage to help support the other strategies on your road to success. Honesty is a great attribute for success.

I'd like to elaborate more on honesty because it's a bonus in your quest to achieve success. It's essential to developing credibility as you strive for your goals, ambitions, and aspirations. The most important thing to remember about honesty is that it's a conscious choice.

You literally should choose to be an honest individual. This may sound easy, but it is not because you can always choose dishonesty, especially if it means instant gratification. Dishonesty carries with it the universal law of karma, which states, "As you do unto others it shall be done unto you." Don't allow dishonesty to be your disposition; it's not worth it. Dishonesty brings a heavy weight upon your conscious mind. This is what happens each time you choose to be dishonest: it's like stacking bricks one on top of another, getting heavier and heavier.

Just like every habit is strengthened by repeating, over time the habit of honesty—or dishonesty—will become a part of you. Do you think you're capable of being an honest person? Deep down inside I think you know the answer to that question. When faced with the choice to be honest or dishonest, what will you choose? It's so easy to choose dishonesty when you want something fast or want an advantage

You must desire to be honest in all your undertaking. This will help you develop an unconscious habit of being honest all the time. Even if you fail in your attempts to be honest, at least you fail with dignity. It takes a tremendous amount of courage to choose honesty over dishonesty. Once it becomes a habit, the decision will be easy.

Let's use Social Security numbers (SSNs) to illustrate this point. Everyone born into American society is assigned a SSN for tracking their activities to verify if they're capable of paying debt in a timely manner. What does this have to do with honesty? Everything. This number literally tracks your ability to be honest when taking the responsibility of assuming credit and debt. Do you uphold legal contracts and agreements? Are you true to your word?

It's important to analyze credit at this point because credit directly represents your ability to resolve debt in a timely manner. Your credit represents your character. **Credit is short for *creditable*.** Your credit is scored on a numbers scale (100 to 1000). The lower your score the less creditable you are, and the higher your score the more creditable you are. You need good credit to buy, rent, borrow, and get better interest rates. An excellent credit score means you have access to anything at a lower interest rate, which means you'll save tons of money.

An excellent credit score sends a positive message to sellers, lenders, creditors, and others. If you're given an opportunity to assume the responsibility of taking on debt, you're a creditable citizen and are accountable for your actions. You really don't want an irresponsible reputation following you wherever you go.

If you choose to get married and have a family, your ability to manage and maintain stability at home may revolve around an honest disposition. Communication, money and sex are the major issue for divorce among married couples.

Therefore, you must be honest about these issues and all issues to maintain trust to hold the family together. You have two paths from which to choose: honesty or dishonesty. One may bring pain for the moment; the other may bring pain for a lifetime. Which will you choose: a rich legacy in honesty, love, caring, or a life of dishonest gain that carries with it the force of failure that is so strong, your conscious thought will punish you for every wrong you commit? You will experience the consequences of your acts, whether they're good or bad; right or wrong. It's up to you. Make sure you weigh your options and choose wisely.

A short story by Patricia Fripp in *A Cup of Chicken Soup for the Soul* illustrates honesty well:

It was a sunny Saturday afternoon in Oklahoma City. My friend and proud father Bobby Lewis was taking his two little boys to play miniature golf. He walked up to the fellow at the ticket counter and said, "How much is it to get in?"

The young man replied, "$3.00 for you and $3.00 for any kid who is older than six. We let them in free if they are six or younger. How old are they?"

Bobby replied, "The lawyer's three and the doctor is seven, so I guess I owe you $6.00."

The man at the ticket counter said, "Hey, Mister, did you just win the lottery or something? You could have saved yourself three bucks. You could have told me that the older one was six; I wouldn't have known the difference."

Bobby replied, "Yes, that may be true, but the kid would have known the difference."

Remember, honesty is always the best policy.

Powerful Quotes about Honesty to Take with You

Understand this law and you will know, beyond
room for the slightest doubt, that you are
constantly punishing yourself for every wrong
you commit and rewarding yourself for every act
of constructive conduct in which you indulge.

—NAPOLEON HILL

I contend that dishonesty will create a failure
force that often manifests itself in other ways,
ways not apparent to the outside observer.

—JOSEPH SUGARMAN

Work joyfully and peacefully, knowing
that right thoughts and right efforts will
inevitably bring about right results.

—JAMES ALLEN

It is better to deserve honors and not have them
than to have them and not deserve them.

—MARK TWAIN

Honesty is the first chapter of the book of wisdom.

—THOMAS JEFFERSON

No legacy is so rich as honesty.

—WILLIAM SHAKESPEARE

HONESTY AFFIRMATIONS

- I AM HONEST AND TRUTHFUL TO MYSELF.
- I AM HONEST BECAUSE I'M WORTHY OF LOVE.
- I AM HONEST BECAUSE I CARE.
- I EXPRESS MYSELF CLEARLY AND HONESTLY.
- I LEARN FROM THE MISTAKES OF THE PAST; I WILL STRIVE TO BE HONEST IN THE FUTURE.
- TODAY I LIVE WITH A HONEST DISPOSITION.
- I HEAL MY SOUL THROUGH HONESTY AND TRUTHFULNESS.
- I LIVE LIFE WITH HONESTY.
- I AM A RIGHTEOUS PERSON.
- I SURROUND MYSELF WITH HONEST PEOPLE.
- I HONESTLY AND EASILY TELL THE TRUTH.
- I TREAT EVERYONE WITH HONESTY AND RESPECT.

IMAGINATION

———◦◦◦◦———

Seeing all possibilities, seeing all that can be done, and how it can be done, marks the power of imagination. Your imagination stands as your own personal laboratory. Here you can rehearse the possibilities, map out plans, and visualize overcoming obstacles. Imagination turns possibilities into reality.

—MOTIVATIONAL QUOTES

MASTER STRATEGY VIII

Imagination

———∞∞∞———

ORVILLE AND WILBUR WRIGHT, BETTER known as the Wright brothers, are note-worthy for using their imagination.

On the morning of December 17, 1903, on the windy dunes at Kitty Hawk in North Carolina, Orville Wright made the first manned and powered flight. Orville and his brother Wilbur operated a bicycle shop in Dayton, Ohio; they had been dreaming about flying since the 1890's. They were not trained scientists or engineers, but they made a scientific study of the problems of flight. They built and tested gliders to understand the principles of flying. They created a wind tunnel in the bicycle shop to test wing designs, and they studied propeller designs and control mechanisms. Their machinist built a 12-horsepower gasoline engine for them. By 1903, the brothers had built a twin-winged airplane, the Flyer, and they felt confident it would fly. At Kitty Hawk, they constructed a wooden track down a hill to provide a smooth surface for takeoff. With Orville at the controls, Wilbur guided the plane down the track, and it bounded into the air. After covering 40 yards in 12 seconds, it landed gently in the sand. Before the day was out, the brothers had made three more flights, one of which lasted almost a minute. Man, at last, had learned to fly.

Imagination is the act or power of forming a mental image of something not present to the senses or never perceived. Imagination and knowledge go hand and hand; they both accentuate the power of the mind. Knowledge is the vast universe that fills your mind which gives you the ability to think, reason, create, remember, fantasize, form opinions, and generate ideas. Imagination is a gateway between fantasy and reality. This is done with pictures, words, numbers, graphs, charts, and so on. Knowledge is the substance that fills the mind that will help generate your universe of imagination or creative mental images (CMI). As Dr. Maxwell Maltz stated, an experience vividly imagined can be as real as the experience itself.

You are directly responsible for building and expanding your imagination. What you put in is what you will get out of it. Use the power of imagination to develop a clear positive success mind-set. Program success into your subconscious thought. Today there is an abundance of resources you can use to train and reprogram your subconscious for success.

This can be done through movies, pictures, affirmations, meditation, hypnosis, and subliminal messages. The process of learning to censor what goes into your subconscious mind is important. When your conscious is cloudy, your ability to focus on the things that matter becomes obscured. To develop a success-conscious mind-set, you must understand the power of conscious, subconscious, and superconscious thinking and how each of them works.

The *conscious* relates to what you're dealing with in the present moment; the *subconscious* stores what you deal with in the present as a record for when you look back on the past. The *superconscious* is the "third eye" used for (CMI) and visualization. It's your help wizard just like the help wizard on a computer, you can use to understand clarify information to see the big picture and become more successful in life. It's your personal workshop to help you organize and navigate you through life. Your imagination is so powerful that you can create a perfect utopia to escape the reality of living in an imperfect world.

The secret key to your imagination is learning how to use it correctly to manifest the things that will bring you closer to achieving your goals, dreams, and aspirations. For example, you can use your imagination to visualize a successful career, relationship, healthy body, financial stability, or anything else that you want to experience in your life. You imagine the finished results and use visualization, which is seeing the process unfold in stages or sequences. By the way, don't put limits on your imagination—because it's infinite.

The power of using the imagination is bigger than anything you can fathom. In your imagination, anything is possible. Where you are doesn't matter; the extent to which you are yourself in your mind's eye. The concept of imagination challenges the core of our belief system. In fact, why choose the least when the world awaits you.

We use imagination to process our next action steps. Imagination has helped us develop this wonderful and magnificent world of technology and information. Besides, everything we now enjoy has been created twice: first in the mind and then in our reality. This is the power of the imagination. Embrace it, and use it to further your goal of becoming a success-driven dynamo.

The universal law of attraction requires the use of the imagination to attract the things you desire into your lifestyle. If you want to manifest the goals and dreams you desire, first you must vividly imagine them in your imagination as reality.

Therefore, the more you think about what you desire in your life, the more you will work to develop a strategy or course of action to make your desires a reality. Do you believe you have the power to manifest the thing you desire? Let me answer that for you: yes, you do! Believe and all things are possible. Remember, your imagination is your help wizard. You can use it to go from outstanding to excellent in the thing you endeavor.

There is no limitation to what you can imagine. Therefore, you should choose the best, the things that will make you happiest. In your imagination practice perfection: see yourself as that excellent sports player, entertainer, CEO, small business entrepreneur, writer, or speaker. Just don't limit yourself.

Let your mind be free to imagine yourself as whatever you want to be. Use your imagination to overcome and conquer fear, failure, setbacks, and shortcomings.

Identify the things that are keeping you from stepping into your greatness. Start now! Replace self-defeating thought patterns with success-driven thoughts. Imagination is the gateway for you to manifest the things you desire; it incites us to create all things. Your future will be brighter than ever through the power of your imagination.

Imagination is the catalyst for creating change. The world would be a much different place without imagination: it's the first step in architecture design, future development, strategic vision, mind mapping for success, writing books, and solving daily problems. Without imagination, the world would be void. Imagination allows humankind to take things that exist in the mind and manifest them into reality.

The imagination is fascinating. Think about all the inventions we enjoy in our world at this moment. At first, they only existed in the form of an idea, lying dormant, waiting to be imagined and brought into existence. I can't fathom the marvelous design and creation that will come in the future. I hope I live long enough to see and experience what the future holds.

In a span of fifty years, we have gone from abstract fuzziness to absolute clarity with TVs. TVs are one of the most reliable sources to alter your state of consciousness. Just look at the experience you have when you watch TV today.

Watching TV totally captivates your imagination and takes you into a fantasy world that is so real it's unbelievable. I don't think people understand the effects of how high-definition (HD), ultra-high definition (UHD), and SUHD TVs will affect the subconscious mind.

People are experiencing an altered state of consciousness and don't realize that it is happening. Remember, whatever you allow into your mind, be it intentional or unintentional, is what your imagination will work with. It's important to know what you want to experience in your life and then intentionally program your mind to match the things you desire.

We are experiencing a new awakening in our conscious thought. I think about our younger generation and how they can't distinguish between fantasy and reality. They can't control their thoughts.

Their minds are bombarded with so much information, and this makes it hard for them to control their thought patterns. If you don't know how to censor what's being programmed into your conscious thoughts, you'll have to deal with it in your sub-conscious mind.

Remember, the subconscious records and stores information and experiences from the conscious. HD, UHD, and S-UHD TVs bypass conscious thought and directly and immediately affect subconscious thought. The imagination can become super powerful thanks to the visual and sound effects that we are dealing with today.

Use the power of your imagination to help develop a sound foundation for success. Use it directly with belief, courage, and desire; they collaborate to form a unified foundation in the pyramid of success. Science says that the universe is continually expanding itself. Your imagination is also continually expanding through knowledge and information. Take initiative to analyze the things you think about daily. Whatever you imagine in your mind, you must believe it's possible if you want to see it in your reality. If you learn to control what you think about, this will help you control the course of your destiny.

Your imagination is an extra sense. Once you understand the power of the imagination, this will make you more conscious about the things that are programmed into your subconscious mind. Your conscious and subconscious mind are confined and limited only if you stop learning.

To adopt a universal mind-set, you must continually expose the mind to knowledge. Albert Einstein was once quoted as saying that imagination is more important than knowledge: "For knowledge is limited to all we now know and understand, while imagination embraces the entire world, and all there ever will be known and understood."

The imagination has unlimited space; this makes it infinite. The imagination is a universe with infinite space. Just as the imagination has played an intricate role in the evolution of humans, you have the power to become aware, to visualize in your mind things you never knew existed. Become your own surrogate and chart a course to help achieve your goals and dreams.

Use your imagination to help create and manifest the things you want in life. Imagination enhances our logical/problem-solving abilities by helping us approach things from different perspectives. To develop a clear, focused imagination, learn how to sift through the information and knowledge you obtain. Suppress and subdue unwanted thoughts that contribute to a cloudy consciousness.

To evoke the wonderful world of your imagination, use idle time for reading, meditating, undergoing hypnosis, using virtual reality, learning a foreign language or musical instrument. If you choose to indulge in substances such as drugs, alcohol, narcotics, hallucinogenics, they can alter your state of consciousness and distract or enhance the imagination.

I refer to the imagination as your mind's eye or third eye. The ability to imagine oneself in a successful state is important as you strive to reach success. If you can't imagine it first, the chances of it becoming a reality are slim to none. In the Bible God used his (CMI) to create the world and to create men and women to inhabit that world. If God is perceived to be all-knowing, we must assume that knowledge is the substance of imagination and came before it.

There would be no imagination without knowledge. The power of the imagination is real. What do you know and believe about the ability of the imagination? Research and learn more about the imagination, because it will play an intricate role in your ability to acquire the things that relate to success and happiness in life.

Use the power of your (CMI) to obtain the things you desire. As I said before, it is your help wizard, but it can't help you if you never learn how to use it. What are you prepared to do? Activate the power of your imagination to manifest the things you desire. Believe without a reasonable doubt that the things you desire are attainable.

Be courageous in pursuit of your dreams, goals, and aspirations. Use your imagination to visually see that car, house, vacation, job, relationship, or other desires of yours. With the right mind-set, develop a strategy to bring it all fruition. Remember, what dominates your thoughts will control your actions. Why not use the power of your imagination to manifest and attract the things you desire?

The mind is all-powerful, functioning like a computer, taking in information from the senses and then storing that information for future use. The key is to program thoughts that directly relate to what you want to achieve. Identify, recognize, and respect the power of the mind. It will help you throughout this life's odyssey we are trapped in. Create balance in life by becoming one with your mind. Don't let the power of the mind dictate and control you. You control it! Our imagination is the key to everything we want, everything we need, and everything we desire. It the bridge between the seen and unseen, between our aspirations and possibilities and our future development.

Your future growth and development directly relates to your ability to use the power of the imagination. You can creatively visualize what your future will be like? When you consider your mind's eye, third eye, or imagination, what do you see? Use your imagination to truly manifest all the things that will bring you success and happiness.

Most of the things that I possess now were manifest by using the universal law of attraction. Using the universal law of attraction, you focus and think about the things you desire, and this will help to manifest them into your reality. I appreciate the power of the imagination because it allows me to see what I desire before it is my reality. Imagination is a creative power to visually see the things you want to manifest in your reality. The things you desire will begin as images in the mind. The creative power of imagination will play an important role in the future development and achievement of success in all professions and career fields.

Powerful Quotes about Imagination to Take with You

The source and center of all man's
creative power is his power of making
images, or the power of imagination.

—**ROBERT COLLIER**

You see things; and you say, "Why?" But I dream
things that never were; and I say, "Why not?

—**GEORGE BERNARD SHAW**

We are told never to cross a bridge till we
come to it, but this world is owned by
men who have "crossed bridges" in their
imagination far ahead of the crowd.

—**SPEAKERS LIBRARY**

For imagination sets the goal "picture" which
our automatic mechanism works on. We act,
or fail to act, not because of "will," as is so
commonly believed, but because of imagination.

—**MAXWELL MALTZ**

Far away there in the sunshine are my highest
aspirations. I may not reach them, but I
can look up and see their beauty, believe in
them, and try to follow where they lead.

—**LOUISA MAY ALCOTT**

First come thought, then organization of that
thought into ideas and plans; then transformation
of those plans into reality. The beginning, as
you will observe, is in your imagination.

—**NAPOLEON HILL**

IMAGINATION AFFIRMATIONS

- MY MIND IS HIGHLY CREATIVE.
- MY IMAGINATION IS EXTREMELY ACTIVE.
- MY MIND IS INFINITE.
- MY MIND IS OPEN TO ALL POSSIBILITIES.
- I GENERATE NEW THOUGHTS AND IDEAS DAILY.
- MY CREATIVITY HAS NO BOUNDS.
- MY IMAGINATION IS LIBERATED.
- I AM NATURALLY A CREATIVE PERSON.
- I HAVE A HIGHLY ACTIVE IMAGINATION.
- MY CREATIVE THOUGHTS AND IDEAS FLOW EFFORTLESSLY.
- MY MIND IS FULL OF INSPIRATION.
- I COMMIT TO DEVELOP MY CREATIVE IMAGINATION.

LOVE

—⚬⚬⚬—

*Love is the most important ingredient of success.
Without it, your life echoes emptiness. With it,
your life vibrates warmth and meaning. Even
in hardship, love shines through. Therefore,
search for love, because if you don't have it,
you're not really living, only breathing.*

—MOTIVATIONAL QUOTES

Love

———∞———

LOVE IS AN INTENSE FEELING of deep affection; it is a feeling of strong or constant affection for a person, place, thing, or idea.

A woman came out of her house and saw three old men with long white beards sitting in her front yard. She did not recognize them. She said, "I don't think I know you, but you must be hungry. Please come in and have something to eat."

"Is the man of the house home?" they asked.

"No," she said. "He's out."

"Then we cannot come in," they replied.

In the evening when her husband came home, she told him what had happened. "Go tell them I am home and invite them in," he said. The woman went out and invited the men in.

"We do not go into a house together, "they replied.

"Why is that?" he wanted to know.

One of the old men explained: "His name is Wealth," he said pointing to one of his friends, and said pointing to another one, "He is Success, and I am Love." Then he added, "Now go in and discuss with your husband which one of us you want in your home."

The woman went in and told her husband what was said. Her husband was overjoyed. "How nice!" he said. "Since that is the case, let us invite Wealth. Let him come and fill our home with wealth!"

His wife disagreed. "My dear, why don't we invite Success?"

Their daughter-in-law was listening from the other corner of the house. She jumped in with her suggestion: "Would it not be better to invite love? Our home will then be filled with love!"

"Let us heed our daughter-in-law's advice," said the husband to his wife. "Go out and invite Love to be our guest."

The woman went out and asked the three old men, "Which one of you is Love? Please come in and be our guest." Love got up and started walking toward the house. The other two also got up and followed him.

Surprised, the lady asked Wealth and Success: "I only invited Love, why are you coming in?"

The old men replied together: "If you had invited Wealth or Success, the other two of us would've stayed out, but since you invited Love, wherever there is love, there is also Wealth and Success!" (Author unknown)

Ask the question: What is love? I can tell you it's hard to explain because the word *love* can relate to a diverse number of separate attitudes, feelings, and states ranging from basic pleasure to intense internal attraction. Love can also refer to intimacy, romance, sex, religion, platonic relationships, or friendship. When you compare it to other emotional states, its diversity of uses makes it unusually hard to define. How you show or relate to love will probably depend on the type of relationship in which you are involved.

What do you believe concerning love? Do you believe love is the universal remedy for the world's problems? I think the lack of love is the key to most of the problems that exist in the world today. Love hasn't been given, shown, or shared enough. Do you agree? We were born for love and happiness. Many people have never experienced true love. The love a mother gives her children to help nurture their existence is one of the greatest of all loves. Unfortunately, we're born in a world turned by lust, bitterness, anger, resentment, conceit, arrogant, narcissism, unhappiness, revenge, and more.

The world has thrown love to the wayside and replaced it with pride, envy, gluttony, lust, anger, greed, and sloth. Well, that's not what we are going to focus on. Instead, you'll learn how to use love as a secret key to unlock your success. Love is success; it's collaborates with honesty, excellence and failure to create leverage at the top of the success pyramid.

Use love to maintain leverage to support the other strategies on your road to success. Love is the emotional intent to manifest the things that will make you happy in life. On your quest to become successful, it is vital that you love yourself and love what you do. It will be one of your biggest challenges on your journey to achieve your dreams. What does love has to do with success? Everything. Nothing can take the place of love. It is love that makes being successful worth it. If you gain the whole world and don't have love, you have attained a lot but might still feel empty.

Goals and achievement are nothing without love. Can you maintain love through it all? That is, through pursing your passion to its completion? As you embark on your journey, love is the one key ingredient that is important to keep with you from start to finish. It makes the experience of pursuing your goals, dreams, and aspirations feel much better; with it you have everything. We achieve success out of love through our talents for self-gratification to help our family and contribute to society.

The heart of all your achievement is love. It's the common denominator for belief, courage, desire, excellence, goal setting, honesty, imagination, failure, persistence, opportunities, and responsibility. Love is the link that ties each of these motivational strategies together to form the powerful force you need to stay motivated and inspired to succeed. Love is a beautiful thing.

Love for some people will become a personal endeavor along with the pursuit of their own success and happiness. Some people substitute the lack of love with material gain in the form of love of money, lust for flesh, the need to control, and the desire for power. The world would be a much better place to live if men could communicate and love one another. Former prime minister Benjamin Disraeli said this about love: "It's the principle of existence and its only end."

Love is power. It's hard to change an old self-defeating behavioral pattern. The power of love will endow you with the ability to overcome challenging situations that you may find yourself in. If you don't know love, try to develop and cultivate love by researching and finding out more about it. You can also extrapolate thoughts from the pass when you experience love from others and practice interjecting the experience in your life. Then read stories and use powerful affirmations to change your method of thinking concerning love. A love affirmation can be repeated to help change your thought about love.

Affirmations of this type would read I'm loving and I'm loving, I'm loving, and I'm loved, I'm loving, and I love it. Take the necessary action that will resonate with your new method of thinking. Through repetition you will alter your state of consciousness. Love will give you the intimate passion and commitment on your road to manifesting and achieving your goals and dreams. Love yourself first and commit to achieving success and happy then apply it to other areas in your life to attain the same results. If you truly want to do what you love and love what you do, develop an intimate unwavering passion and commitment to make your goals and dreams a reality. Happiness is found in the manifestation of the thoughts. Get intimate with what you dream about and make your quest for success a personal mission. Throw your heart into it, and everything else will follow. Love will endow you with the strength to be courageous and will help you develop a burning desire. This will move you and motivate you to act. Persist until the door of success opens wide and tells you to come in, but you first must love what you are doing.

Love is taking the opportunity to be honest with yourself and other people. Integrity has its place in success. In fact, it is vital for success. Don't be afraid or ashamed to have an honest character centered on love. Honesty is still your best policy. Love is taking responsibility for yourself and others. Hold yourself accountable for the things pertaining to success and achievement that don't get accomplished. It's easy to blame others for our setbacks, failures, and shortcomings. You are the only one responsible for achieving your goals and dreams, no one else.

Just remember, failure should be a motivating factor that can help prepare you for success. Love yourself and love what you do: this is what can help you to go beyond an average effort to achieve your goals, dreams, and aspirations. Committed passion will makes you go the extra mile for what you want. To reach higher for the things you want in life, you should be committed, passionate, and confident in the possibilities. Excellence speaks for itself.

Use love to help achieve your goals and dreams. Are you willing to stay the course and see it all unfold and come to fruition? Think about that wonderful feeling you'll get when you experience success in all areas of your life. Now you'll have all the time in the world to spend quality time with family and friends; take that dream vacation; resolve personal issues; or just have an attitude of gratitude for all the things that have brought you love, success, and happiness. This is the genuine love that you can experience when you create balance by using these key characteristics to help you manifest all the things that pertain to success and happiness. I must say love and happiness are hard to attain. You should choose love and happiness by lining your lifestyle up with what you want and desire.

In conclusion, I'd like to reiterate the true value and importance of love. Love is the pinnacle and reigns paramount wherever you go and whatever you do. Tap into universal love, the greatest love that exists. Always strive to do better as your life's odyssey unfolds. Find what gives your life meaning; that's why you are here, to live your best life. Marvel at the wonders of the world, but learn to appreciate the simple things about life, as that's love. It's the love for life that helps to make you unstoppable, makes you want to go the extra mile to do things for yourself or others. It's important that you love yourself and love what you do because as you make bold moves in life, you are going to be tested. Just as the story at the beginning of this chapter showed, you should invite love into your life and home. Once you grant love the opportunity to come in, everything else will line up perfectly and follow. **Let love in! Let love in! Let love in!**

The key to living a longer, healthier, happier, and more successful life is to learn how to love. Love is life; when you learn to love, you will learn to live. Love is the greatest of all the key characteristics in this book. When you reach the end of your life's journey, will love reign supreme?

It's important that when you look back later you can say that you gave love, experienced love, and most of all, loved yourself. Will you be able to release, relax, and let go of it all, knowing you did your very best through the power of love? Love should play an integral part in the things you achieve in life. I could sit here and write about love from now until end of the world, and I still wouldn't have placed enough emphasis on the power or importance of love.

Love is imperative to the existence of humanity. Nonetheless, men can't live in peace with one another because they don't know how to love and respect one another. Once we learn how to love, we will learn to live a more fulfilled life.

The best part of all our lives will be realized once we cultivate and activate the power of love.

Lydia Marie Childs said, "The cure for all the ills and wrongs, the cares, the sorrows and crimes of humanity, all lie in one word, 'love.' It is the divine vitality that everywhere produces and restores life." The world will be transformed.

Love in all its depth, delight, and ecstasy will survive and reign supreme long after all has perished and ceased to exist. Love is immortal, life flourishes in abundance with it, and no force is more powerful than it. So, hold fast to love and let it transform you.

Powerful Quotes about Love to Take with You

The moment you have in your heart this extraordinary thing called love and feel the depth, the delight, the ecstasy of it, you will discover that for you the world is transformed.

—J. KRISHNAMURTI

You will find as you look back upon your life that the moments when you have really lived, are the moments when you have done things in a spirit of love.

—HENRY DRUMMOND

We are all born for love. It is the principle of existence, and its only end.

—BENJAMIN DISRAELI

Love is everything. It is the key to life, and its
influences are those that move the world.

—Ralph Waldo Trine

Where there is love there is life. . .

—Mohandas Gandhi

Love is life . . . And if you miss love, you miss life.

—Leo Guscaglia

LOVE AFFIRMATIONS

- I AM A MANIFESTATION OF LOVE.
- LOVE IS MY PATHWAY FOR CHANGE.
- I WELCOME LOVE INTO MY LIFE.
- TODAY IS BEGINNING OF A NEW CYCLE OF LOVE.
- I BELIEVE IN THE POWER OF LOVE.
- I AM LOVING AND LOVED BY MANY.
- I WELCOME THE OPPORTUNITY TO LOVE.
- TODAY, I AM MET WITH UNEXPECTED LOVE AND JOY.
- I AM OVERFLOWING WITH LOVE, JOY AND HAPPINESS.
- I TAP INTO THE DIVINE POWER OF UNIVERSAL LOVE.
- MY MIND HAS TRANSCEND, MY HEART HAS PEACE, AND MY SOUL IS TRANQUIL.
- I WILL USE LOVE TO CO-ORDINATE MY MIND, BODY AND SPIRIT.

OPPORTUNITY

───⋘───

There are no limits to our opportunities. Most of us see only a small portion of what is possible. We create opportunities by seeing the possibilities, and having the persistence to act upon them. We must always remember, opportunities are always here, but we must look for them.

—Motivational Quotes

Opportunity

———⊶⊷———

THE FIRST FLAG WAS ADOPTED by the new United States of America on June 14, 1777 but no one knows who really design it. That first flag had 13 stars and 13 stripes, representing the original states of the Union. The colors red, white and blue were borrowed from the British flag, symbolizing the country's English heritage. Additional stripes and new stars were added when Vermont and Kentucky joined the Union, but in 1818, Congress decided to return to 13 stripes to honor the original states, anticipating the addition of a new star for each new state. The current flag, with its 50 stars, was adopted in 1960 after Hawaii gained statehood. There are many names for the American flag, such as "Old Glory," the Star-Spangled Banner," and "the Stars and Stripes." It remains a symbol of democracy and freedom wherever it is unfurled.

America is deemed as the land of opportunity, where anyone can achieve anything he or she puts their mind to, no matter who they are or where they come from. Although slaves were brought here against their will, after suffering years of mental and physical abuse, there are men and women of such background that have turned out great despite the challenges they faced.

It's always those who take advantage of opportunities who will grow and make progress in life. America has given All Americans an opportunity for a better way of life. Everyone has immigrated to America for better opportunities.

People from Europe, the Middle East, South America, Asia, and other parts of the world all come to America, the land of opportunity. Immigrants have made a considerable contribution to this country. They hold a wide variety of professions and skills. Many still observe the customs and practices of their culture. Slowly but surely America has changed for the better to accommodate the needs of all who reside here. We all need to recognize the fact that evolution doesn't happen overnight. It's a gradual and consistent process.

An opportunity is defined as a set of circumstances that makes it possible to do something. Opportunity is everywhere, but it always up to us, our responsibility, to see them and take advantage of them. The question is, how do you line up or position yourself to be more receptive to opportunities or to recognize them when they present themselves? Opportunity will not knock at your door; you should knock at opportunity's door. However, even if it does knock, it may be very soft, which means you need to be paying attention. Program yourself to be open and receptive to opportunities.

You can program and empower yourself to recognize and take advantage of opportunities by staying up to date. Opportunity is part of creating formation on the pyramid of success. Finding the favorable or advantageous circumstance or suitable time is what will catapult you through the doors of success. Taking advantage of opportunities is about staying ready.

How ready are you if you should get an opportunity now? Use the power of strategic planning to look at external factors that will affect you now and in the future. By having an open mind, you will be more receptive to opportunities that become available, and you'll be ready to respond in a more positive manner. Learning how to analyze strategically is a high-level skill that will help you think about your long-term plans. It teaches you to break down intricate and complex issues into more manageable pieces.

The focus is on the external factors because the outside factors have a powerful influence on you. You will learn that you can manage your responses to these influences instead of believing there are no alternative solutions. Strategic planning will help you anticipate what might happen, evaluate how likely it is to happen, and prepare for it to happen. It will secure your future as you will be better prepared for what might happen. It will also help you develop clearer, more appropriate goals and help you make better-quality decisions.

When you understand the influence from the outside world, you can make better decisions in the future. This will keep you on the fast track to success.

The ability to analyze your external environment is a key step to strategic planning and being prepared for opportunities. Strategic analysis will reinforce your chances of achieving your goals and dreams because you will prepare better by allocating resources for future purposes. The cost of not doing some form of strategic planning can be a missed opportunity.

Opportunities will not always be favorable, advantageous, convenient, or timely. You need to learn how to create opportunity. Remember, opportunity is not necessarily going to show up and say, "Here I am." Knowing your worth plays a vital role in this process. Anything you undertake or embark on has the potential to be new opportunity. Therefore, stay open and ready to take advantage of the given situation.

Sometimes opportunities that will benefit you may not even look like opportunities. The ability to recognize opportunity is a crucial step when you start your quest to manifest abundance in your life. Your major objective is to be successful, however; if you are to make the best of any opportunity, it's important to view opportunity with an optimistic mind-set. The more positive you are, the more favorable the opportunity will turn out to be. Even if it is not a grand opportunity, remember that small chances can lead to something bigger that could substantially increase your chances of success—and even your net worth—beyond your wildest dreams. It doesn't matter what your goals and dreams are; learning to take advantage of opportunity will help you to create the life you're destined to enjoy. Ask yourself some basic questions: What are the benefits of implementing a success opportunity strategy? Will there be any adverse effects from implementing the strategy, and are the results worth making the changes?

The major reason for conducting a success opportunity analysis is to recognize the benefits changes will bring. For example, if you decide to broaden your business by offering a specific new product alongside your services, the benefit may be that you will meet another need your current customers have, and now they will purchase the new product along with your services, increasing your profit. In the analysis, you would look closely at what expense would be involved in adjusting the production process, designing the packaging, and pricing the products to be competitive in the marketplace.

If it is determined that the associated costs can be offset by the sale of the products and earn a profit for you, there is a good chance that this opportunity is worth pursuing. Putting yourself in the know makes it easier to create more opportunity for yourself.

Success opportunity strategy must look at the long-range effects associated with the change that is being considered. This means not only looking at issues of production and cost, but also intangible factors. If adding products to the production process means that customers can't buy the services they want, then they will likely take their business somewhere else. This action undermines not only the profits from services but also reduces the consumer market for products. The change would have a negative effect on profit accumulation over the long-term and wouldn't be worth the effort.

To help manifest success and create abundance in your life, use SWOT analysis to understand your personal *Strengths, Weaknesses, Opportunities,* and *Threats.* By knowing your SWOT, you'll better position yourself to succeed. By using your talents effectively, you can avoid some of the simple pitfalls of life, but when you know your SWOT as well the chances of succeeding in all that you do increase dramatically.

To explain, *strengths* are your positive attributes or traits that give you a comparative boost or even a competitive edge in terms of manifesting goals and dreams. If the goal is to get a job with a six-figure income, the strengths you'll need may include great communication skills, a strong work ethic, flexibility and adaptability, problem-solving skills, the ability to be a team player, self-discipline, and the list goes on. Your strengths are the things that will help you to become your best.

Weakness represents lack of or opposite of the personal traits and characteristics that would benefit your pursuit of success and happiness. These traits can include the following:

procrastination; taking things personally; impatient and poor communication; a lack of self-discipline, self-esteem, or motivation; indecisiveness; shyness, and the like. It's important to develop the traits that will help you to seize opportunities when they present themselves. Stay ready, and if there are traits you know you need to work on to increase your chances of becoming more successful, start working on them before you really need them.

Remember, *opportunities* are everywhere, but you'll have to be prepared and ready at any moment to capitalize on them. If you want to position yourself for success, take advantage of conferences, workshops, free educational training, classes, networking with successful people in your field—put yourself out there, and do whatever it takes to meet your appointment with success. If you want success, then success wants you: it's the natural universal law of attraction. Apply it to your lifestyle and make it happen.

Lastly, *threats* represent those external factors that negatively prevent you from achieving the things you want out of life. Learn how to recognize threats, but don't waste a lot of time and energy worrying about them. Threats can do you no harm unless you allow them to. You may not be able to control everything, but you always have control over how you respond to whatever happens in your life.

Focus only on the positive, release, relax, and let go of all fears about threats that have the potential to hinder your effort to reach or achieve your goals and aspirations. Use the combined power of your mind, body, and spirit to overcome and conquer anything that prevents your pursuit of happiness.

Opportunity will always exist in many forms. Are you open and receptive to recognize an opportunity? Have you aligned yourself to take advantage of opportunities when they present themselves? Opportunity doesn't always knock on your door; you may have to knock on opportunity's door. George Bernard Shaw said, "The people who get on in this world are the people who get up and look for the circumstances they want, and if they can't find them, make them."

You hold the keys to all the opportunities that come into your life. This is the one key concept you need to understand. Your success, happiness, and achievement depend on you. There is power lying latent within you waiting to be discovered. Open your eyes and take advantage of this power. Remember, any situation when perceived properly becomes an opportunity. Opportunity is a gold key for you to seek the potential to create and manifest the things that make your life more fulfilling. You are the opportunity you seek. You have the power. You are endowed with the ability to develop opportunities that are waiting to be discovered. Your great success story is waiting for you to recognize and take the opportunity to make it happen.

Powerful Quotes about Opportunity to Take with You

Opportunities, they are all around us. There
is power lying latent everywhere waiting
for the observant eye to discover it.

—Orison Swett Marden

Most successful men have not achieved their
distinction by having some new talent or
opportunity presented to them. They have
developed the opportunity that was at hand.

—Bruce Barton

The people who get on in this world are the people
who get up and look for the circumstances they
want, and, if they can't find them, make them.

—George Bernard Shaw

Opportunity, often it comes disguised in the
form of misfortune or temporary defeat.

—**NAPOLEON HILL**

Opportunity rarely knocks on your
door. Knock rather on opportunity's
door if you ardently wish to enter.

—**B. C. FORBES**

A wise man will make more
opportunities than he finds.

—**ALBERT EINSTEIN**

OPPORTUNITY AFFIRMATIONS

* I OPEN MY MIND TO THE ENDLESS POSSIBILITY OF OPPORTUNITIES.
* I AM OPEN TO NEW OPPORTUNIIES TO ACHIEVE GREATNESS.
* I MAKE PRESENT WONDROUS NEW IDEAS OF POSSIBILITIES.
* I MAKE CREATIVE NEW OPPORTUNIITIES IN MY LIFE.
* EVERY DAY IS A NEW OPPORTUNITY TO EXPRESS MY TRUE TALENTS.
* I ATTRACT NEW OPPORTUNITIES TO EXPRESS MY UNIQUENESS.
* EVERY OPPORTUNITY HAS THE POTENTIAL TO BRING GREATER POSSIBILITIES.
* I TAKE ACTION TO CREATE NEW OPPORTUNITIES.
* NEW OPPORTUNITIES APPEAR BEFORE ME DAILY.
* OBSTACLES ARE OPPORTUNITIES IN DISQUISE.
* WHEREVER I GO OPPORTUNITY WILL FOLLOW.
* I COMMIT TO ACT ON ALL OPPORTUNITIES AS THEY PRESENT THEMSELVES.

PERSISTENCE

The power to hold on in spite of everything, the power to endure, this is the winner's quality. Persistence is the ability to face defeat again and again without giving up, to push on in the face of great difficulty, knowing that victory can be yours. Persistence means taking pains to overcome every obstacle and do what's necessary to reach your goals.

—MOTIVATIONAL QUOTES

Persistence

———⊗∞⊗———

PERSISTENCE IS THE ACTION OR fact of persisting; the quality or state of being persistent; especially perseverance. Are you willing to stay the course despite difficulties or opposition? It is important that you stay persistent because that's the only way to reach your goal. That means no matter how you feel, and on those days, you do not feel as motivated as you would want, you must still get up and give life your best shot.

Remember, quitting is not an option, and if you want to get the result you want, you must persist. It's the truth: you never want to give up on something that you can't go a day without thinking about. What would you like to achieve? Achieving it may not be easy, but it's possible once you are willing to persist.

Thomas Edison is an icon of persistence. He was noteworthy for trying a whopping one thousand times before finding the filament for the light bulb. Edison was a prolific inventor, holding

1,093 US patents in his name, as well as many patents in the United Kingdom, France, and Germany. More significant than the number of Edison's patents was the widespread impact of his inventions: electric light and power utilities, sound recording and motion pictures all established major new industries world-wide. Edison's inventions contributed to mass communication and, in particular, telecommunications. These included a stock ticker, a mechanical vote recorder, a battery for an electric car, electrical power, recorded music, and motion pictures. His advanced work in these fields was an outgrowth of his early career as a telegraph operator. Edison developed a system of electric-power generation and distribution to homes, businesses, and factories. His first power station on Pearl Street in Manhattan, New York, was a crucial development in the modern industrialized world. I used Thomas Edison as an example because his persistence and determination were powerfully present in his life. (Wikipedia)

Since the dawn of time, men have continued to exist through knowledge and development. We have persevered to keep endeavoring as human beings. Man is a fine example of persistence. We have continued generation after generation, forever evolving as time makes change inevitable.

Now I'd like to share with you the greatest example of persistence: time. Time will continue long after we are deceased. Time is the reason for everything; without time nothing would exist. Time is the alpha and omega, and all things brought into existence are because of time. Great dynasties and empires have been built, but none have withstood the test of time. Time gives birth to all things then watches them grow, develop, mature, decline, and die. Time is the ultimate avenger and healer, yet it is not biased. Learn how to master time and use it wisely. Become one with time, and time won't exist for you anymore. What I mean is you let go of the past, stay current with the present and embrace change so that you're prepared for the future. Master time, and you will be able to overcome and conquer all of life's issues and situations.

Do you believe in your own ability to manifest the things you desire? Before you'll be able to persist, you'll have to believe you can. The magnitude of your belief will play an intricate role in your ability to achieve all the things you desire. A strong belief system is the foundation for persistence. The level of your belief will determine the lengths you will go to make those goals, dreams, and aspirations a reality. You must initiate the power of persistence, but it is your belief system that is going to help you to push through. It is also important that you use your imagination to maintain a clear image of the goals and dreams you set forth. If you can clearly see what you want without having it, you'll be more likely to find the strength within you to go after it. Desire will keep you motivated and inspired to persist in achieving success and happiness.

Do you want to achieve your goals? However, to achieve your goals you'll have to push yourself, so there are strategies included in this book that can help you to develop persistence. Let them work together to help you meet your need to be more successful.

Persist with unwavering courage. Why? What you desire out of life depends on it. The more action you take, the less fearful you'll be. Through banishing your fears, you'll develop faith in what you desire, and with faith comes courage. What you don't want to do is allow the bumps in the road to stop you from achieving your dreams. If you fall, get back up; you have it within you to do so. Persist and build confidence and self-esteem. Remember that all the things you desire, desire you. Use the universal law of attraction because what you move toward will move toward you.

No matter what it takes, visualize what you want to achieve. Why? Imagination can help you vividly experience the manifestation of your desires as if they are real. What does this have to do with persistence? Everything, because this is how you continually maintain clear focus.

If you persist with clarity and focus, your goals and dreams are more likely to be realized. This is all a part of the big picture, of how to bring it together. It's easier to go after what you can see yourself accomplishing. Like a jigsaw puzzle, until all the pieces come together the picture of your success will remain separate, unidentified pieces.

Once all the pieces fall into place and you have a clear view of the big picture. If you have what it takes to persist, you'll put the pieces together. Just don't stop until you do. Besides, there are people watching you who are inspired by you and the action you are taking. Keep pressing forward, and if what you are pursuing is something that you cannot go a day without thinking about, never give up. You already know that being persistent always pays off when you can creatively visualize the big picture and then set the right goals.

Goals are the pieces that will bring the big picture into reality. Take, for example, when you go on a strict diet and exercise program—persistence is necessary to make it work. As you see the fat and pounds burn away from acting on your goals, you'll have more energy, and your clothes will be looser. Being persistent is a part of being excellent, as it often requires going beyond the call of duty, doing more than what others expect.

Remember, only some people will persist. Will you be a part of those who do? If you're growing at all as a human being, then you're going to be a little different from who you were the previous year. And if you consciously pursue personal development, the changes will often be dramatic and rapid.

There is no guarantee that the goals you set today will still be the ones you'll want to achieve five or ten years from now. Learn how to evaluate your progress and the goals you set for yourself. Make sure they are up-to-date and correct. Proper management and maintenance of goals is a must. If you buy a computer and use it over a period of time, the computer will get infected with viruses, cookies, pop-ups, spam, and other issues.

It is important to run the maintenance program to remove all unused programs, so the computer will function properly. If the way you are trying to reach your goals doesn't work, you can always try other ways that may help you more. Besides, just like a computer, you too must remove what's not working for you, things that may end up distracting you. I'm holding on to goals and dreams I've had for almost fifteen years—that's just to say: don't let setbacks stop you from pursuing your goals. My goals are still relative now and are about to come fruition. They still motivate and inspire me. They aren't out of date, and I believe they will happen soon. You are dynamic, and your goals should be too.

One thing to consider before you start diversifying your goals is to make sure you complete the goals you already have. Doing so will prevent you from feeling overwhelmed. Get an accountability partner to help you stay the course until you finish. You may have to develop a persistent attitude by any means necessary. Just to let you know, worrying about your goals is not going to help you to accomplish them; only acting on them will.

Some goals take time to manifest, and it's for that reason you need to throw your heart into making it happen. You should manage your time the best you can. You cannot allow unnecessary things to take up most of your time.

Persist! Persist! Persist! Don't stop; never give up. You've got what it takes to achieve your goals. Should I say it again? You have what it takes. Remember, if you can see the result in your mind's eye, it will be much easier to go after it because you've already visualized it. It's hard to hit a target you cannot see. Vision will motivate and inspire you to be more persistent and consistent in your actions.

This is what will help you consistently get the results you want. What is it going to be? Will you persist despite challenges, or are you going to quit before you achieve your goal? I know you are going to persist. I know you are going to go after your goals as if your life depends on it, and the truth is, it does. Winners win because they refuse to let their failures defeat them. Success will only release its reward when you refuse to quit trying to succeed. Don't give up because you may be one yard from the winning touchdown. Use the power of persistence to overcome and conquer all obstacles that come your way. Remember to stick with it to the bitter end because time will bring all great achievements to pass.

Powerful Quotes about Persistence to Take with You

I do not think there is any other quality
so essential to success of any kind as the
quality of perseverance. It overcomes
almost everything, even nature.

—JOHN D. ROCKEFELLER

What this power is I cannot say; all I know is
that it exists and it becomes available only
when a man is in that state of mind in which
he knows exactly what he wants and is fully
determined not to quit until he finds it.

—ALEXANDER GRAHAM BELL

The majority of men meet with failure because
of their lack of persistence in creating new
plans to take the place of those which fail.

—NAPOLEON HILL

Most people give up just when they're about to achieve success. They quit on the one-yard line. They give up at the last minute of the game one foot from a winning touchdown.

—H. ROSS PEROT

Success is failure turned inside out. The silver tint of the clouds of doubt and you never can tell how close you are. It may be near when it seems so far, so stick to the fight when you're hardest hit. It's when things seem worse, that you must not quit.

—UNKNOWN

PERSISTENCE AFFIRMATIONS

* I GAIN STRENGTH AND DETERMINATION TO CONTINUE, BY REFUSING FAILURE.
* EVERY CHALLENGE I FACE, GIVE ME MORE DETERMINATION.
* I AM MORE DETERMINED THAN EVER TO ACHIEVE MY GOALS.
* I PUSH MYSELF TO GO A LITTLE FURTHER EVERY DAY.
* EVERY DAY I DEVELOP AN ADAMANT DRIVE AND DETERMINATION TO SUCCEED.
* I STRIVE TO GIVE EVERY TASK MY BEST EFFORT.
* I AM DETERMINED TO ACCOMPLISH MY GOALS.
* I ADAMANTLY COMMIT TO PERSIST UNTIL I SUCCEED.
* I PERSIST TO ACHIEVE GREAT THINGS.
* I PERSIST TO BE SUCCESSFUL IN ALL THAT I DO.
* I PERSIST TO GO FUTHER EACH DAY.
* I PERSIST TO BE SUCCESSFUL.

RESPONSIBILITY

—⟨⟨⟨⟩⟩⟩—

*The fulfillment of your dreams lies within you
and you alone. When you understand and
accept this, then nothing, or no one, can deny
you greatness. The power to succeed or fail
is yours. And no one can take that away.*

—MOTIVATIONAL QUOTES

Responsibility

⸺⸺ ❧ ⸺⸺

RESPONSIBILITY IS THE QUALITY OR state of being responsible: such as; moral, legal, or mental accountability. Now, let me share with you a short story that sums up the quality of taking responsibility.

The Power of Responsibility: It's been said that the line between childhood and adulthood is crossed when we move from saying 'It got lost' to 'I lost it'. Indeed, being accountable and understanding and accepting the role our choices play in the things that happen are crucial signs of emotional and moral maturity. That's why responsibility is one of the main pillars of good character. Many people have been seduced by the Peter Pan philosophy of refusing to grow up and avoiding the burdens implied in being accountable. Yes, responsibility sometimes requires us to do things that are unpleasant or even frightening. It asks us to carry our own weight, prepare and set goals, and exercise the discipline to reach our aspirations. But the benefits of accepting responsibility far outweigh the short-lived advantages of refusing to do so. No one makes his or her life better by avoiding responsibility. In fact, irresponsibility is a form of self-imposed servitude to circumstances and to other people. Responsibility is about our ability to respond to circumstances and to choose the attitudes, actions, and reactions that shape our lives. It is a concept of power that puts us in the driver's seat. The grand panorama of the potential of our live can only be appreciated when we begin to be accountable and self-reliant. Responsible people not only depend on themselves, but show others that they can be depended on. This breeds trust, and trust is a key that opens many doors. If you want more control over your life and the pleasures, prerogatives, and power of freedom and independence, all you have to do is be responsible.

"Michael Josephson"

Taking 100 percent responsibility is one of the strategies of success. Besides, if there is something that you want to accomplish, no one should be more passionate than you. To enjoy all that's possible for you, you will have to be accountable for your actions. For example, the pilot of a plane, the conductor of a train, the captain of a ship, or the driver of a car all have one thing in common: responsibility. They are all responsible for the safe navigation and destination of their vehicles. By taking responsibility, you become the pilot, conductor, captain, and driver of your life; you believe in your ability to control your own destiny to fulfill your dreams.

In truth, the things you do daily are taking you somewhere, and you can choose where that destination is instead of allowing circumstances to dictate how things turn out for you. If you don't control the plot or course of your own life, someone else will. You will find yourself as a bystander, watching your life's script being directed by someone else. Don't just let that happen. Be your own director so the outcome will be what you want. Taking responsibility will help you to explore more of life and in turn will make life more fulfilling. Being responsible for your actions is what's going to make the difference.

If you leave your success or happiness to someone else, you may not experience either. Success and happiness are directly related to your ability to take responsibility for the life you live. You are compelled to act when you decide to be responsible for your choices. It is easy to think or believe you're the victim of circumstances. You have the power to change your situation and the circumstances that occur in your life.

No matter what, you can choose to stay positive and optimistic through it all. Believe in yourself—that is very important—and take responsibility so you can be a positive example for other people who may think they cannot get out of the situation they are in. I want you to know that if you have a sound mind, body, and spirit, thank God, and keep striving for success and happiness.

Wherever you are in life now is due to your choices. Hindsight is twenty-twenty, but never look back in regret. Why not? Because the past cannot be changed. Keep going forward, take responsibility as you do, and do the best you possibly can in the future. The only thing that truly matters is the present and what you do to make your future what you want it to be. What you do going forward is what matters most. Let the past go, focus on the present, and prepare for the future. We are not promised tomorrow, but what if it comes and you have done nothing to enhance the whole person you are? Every second, minute, hour, day, month, and year that goes by is gone; it isn't retrievable. That time is lost forever. Remember, you will never get that time back, so make the most of it while it's at your disposal.

You only make choices according to what you know and your ability to analyze the outcome of the choices you're considering. If there is something you want to know or learn, it's your responsibility to seek it out. Remember, what you seek, you will find.

Taking responsibility for yourself means actively accepting the fact that your experiences in life are related to how you think, feel, and behave. If you are not happy at this point in your life, you can always change your course. If you truly want to take responsibility, it may require changing how you think and what you believe. Make your desire to achieve your goals and dreams consistent with how you think.

Remember to discard all thoughts that are not helping you to grow and achieve the things that you desire in life. One thing that you can do to reprogram your mind is to use affirmations, subliminal audio messages, and helpful books. Doing so will help you reinvent your thoughts, and you'll start to view every event in your life as a stepping-stone toward taking total responsibility for yourself.

It's your duty, your responsibility, and your obligation to fulfill your need and desire to manifest the things you want in life. You will need to take full responsibility—100 percent—to stay committed and to fulfill that commitment. The doorway that leads to happiness and success is waiting for you to walk through it. What are you prepared to do? Don't let it slip away. Stand up, take responsibility, and make it happen. You are in control of your destiny.

Take an honest look at where you are in life. It doesn't matter what your situation is now. You are responsible for how you think, so act in accordance with what you want to achieve. Remember, you cannot change what has happened, and sometimes things happen out of your control. But even with those things, how you respond is always in your control. Don't blame anyone for your present condition; as you go forward with your life, make sure you forgive everyone who has hurt or disappointed you.

Take 100 percent responsibility for yourself now. You have the power to make your life exactly what you want it to be. You can't accomplish anything by worrying about things you have no control over. Taking responsibility for your life can be a challenge, but you can do it. It's worth the effort, and the more you practice taking responsibility, the better you get at it. Don't leave what you want to chance. Take charge, and take charge now! This is the starting point for you to achieve great things in your life. Stay proactive as you pursue your goals and dreams in life. Successful people take control of their destiny. They create the things in life that will lead to happiness. They know their present reflects something they did in the past. They don't blame family, friends, or external factors for the way life is. Unsuccessful people blame everything and everybody for their failures and shortcomings.

Accepting responsibility gives you direct control over your condition. Successful people accept the good and bad as they continually resolve issues that occur in their lives. They continue to move forward with optimism and enthusiasm and at the same time find ways to stay motivated and inspired.

In closing, just remember you are the primary source of all things that manifest in your life. Taking responsibility will give you the power to control your destiny and be successful in life. It will give you a sense of confidence and self-esteem. Relax, release, and let go of anything that binds you from achieving the things you want in life. You can have all the things you desire if you would just believe that it is possible. You create your past and future now in the present.

Make sure you manifest only the things that will lead to a happy, healthy, and fulfilling life. You are the boss. Success requires you to accept responsibility for your existence. You are responsible for the outcome of your future. The measure of your success depends on you. Let this motivate and inspire you to be your absolute best. Successful people take responsibility: it's the quality that distinguishes them from those who are not.

Arnold J. Toynbee said, "As human beings, we are endowed with freedom of choice, and we cannot shuffle off our responsibility upon the shoulders of God or nature. We must shoulder it ourselves. It is up to us." Use the power of responsibility: it's a key concept that will help you create and achieve the things that will lead to success and happiness. **You were born to be a success, but first you must recognize and accept that fact—then act on it.**

Powerful Quotes about responsibility to Take with You

There is a kind of elevation which does not depend on fortune; it is a certain air which distinguishes us, and seems to destine us for great things; it is a price which we imperceptibly set upon ourselves.

—FRANCOIS DE LA ROCHEFOUCAULD

Success on any major scale requires you to accept responsibility. In the final analysis, the one quality that all successful people have is the ability to take on responsibility.

—MICHAEL KORDA

Some men have thousands of reasons why they cannot do what they want to, when all they need is one reason why they can.

—WILLIS R. WHITNEY

I was taught very early that I would have
to depend entirely upon myself; that
my future lay in my own hands.

—DARIUS OGDEN MILLS

Hold yourself responsible for a higher
standard than anybody else expects
of you. Never excuse yourself.

—Henry Ward Beecher

Nothing happens by itself. It all will come your
way, once you understand that you have to
make it come your way, by your own exertions.

—BEN STEIN

RESPONSIBILITY AFFIRMATIONS

* I TAKE 100% RESPONSIBILITY FOR MY LIFE.
* I TAKE RESPONSIBILITY FOR MY THOUGHTS, BELIEFS, WORDS AND ACTIONS.
* I AM RESPONSIBLE FOR WHAT HAPPEN TO ME IN LIFE.
* I TAKE RESPONSIBILITY WITH PRIDE.
* MY COMMITMENT TO BE RESPONSIBLE DEFINES ME.
* MY ACHIEVEMENTS FOR BEING RESPONSIBLE MAKE ME OPTIMISTIC.
* I TAKE RESPONSIBILITY TO EMPOWER MY LIFE.
* I WEAR MY RESPONSIBILITY BADGE WITH DIGNITY.
* I COMMIT TO TAKE RESPONSIBILITY FOR MY LIFE NOW.
* I TAKE RESPONSIBILITY TO LIBERATE MYSELF FROM BAD HABITS.
* I TAKE RESPONSIBILITY TO INIATE, ACTIVATE, ENGAGE AND IMPLEMENT A NEW LIFE.
* I COMMIT TO BE A MORE RESPONSIBLE PERSON IN THE FUTURE.

CONCLUSION

———⊗∞⊗———

LIFE IS AN ODYSSEY; A fantastic voyage of discovery. Life is dynamic, forever evolving and changing; it makes no guarantees and owes us nothing. Despite where you've come from, as you evolve and arrive at the age of understanding or enlightenment, you must prepare to take control of your own existence. Your journey begins at the age of understanding. You must recognize the importance of acquiring knowledge and then applying it so that your life's odyssey will be exactly as you plan. Your adventure will only be conceivable if you use knowledge wisely to help you manifest and achieve the things you want in life. Have the courage to believe in your own ability to make things happen. Develop a burning desire for success, then manifest the things that will make you happy. You are responsible for taking control of your life; don't put it on anyone else's shoulders.

Knowledge is what will give you that power. I keep stressing knowledge because it's the key, but you must learn how to use it to get the things you desire from life. It's the key that will help you develop the belief that all things are possible; it will teach you to use your imagination to visualize what you want so you can set goals and achieve them. Your quest is to use knowledge to help you change and stay current with time. Implement excellence along the way; this will keep you a step above the rest. Activate the power of love and honesty to maintain integrity. Persist and don't worry about failure. Who you are and what you become in life depends on your ability to utilize the knowledge you acquire. Read this book and let it help you make the necessary changes in your life so that you can rise to your full potential. This book is worth reading repeatedly. Share it with your friends and family. You are destined for greatness, and the strategies within this book will help you tap into that greatness. Every day is one of endless possibilities—you should embrace it and treat it as if it were more precious than silver or gold. I've shared with you exactly what you need to become excellent at whatever you undertake. I hope you will use and cherish these strategies for a lifetime.

HOW TO USE THE SUCCESS MASTER STRATEGIES

———— ∞ ————

THROUGHOUT THIS BOOK, I'VE MENTION The Success Pyramid. Now I'd like to take this opportunity to explain what this means. The Success Pyramid consist of grouping the strategies together to build a pyramid, so they will work more effectively for you: Use Belief, Imagination, Goals, and Desire together to create a solid foundation. Use Courage, Responsibility, Persistence and failure are used together to develop formation. Love, Honesty, Excellence and Opportunity are what you use to create leverage to hold everything together. Group them in how ever order that works best for you. You can also use them consecutively in the order that will work for you. It doesn't matter how you use them, just commit them to memory. When you are faced with adversity, doubt and uncertainty; use these strategies to help you make good decisions about your life.

REFERENCES

© 1984 By GREAT QUOTATIONS INC.

© Grolier Inc. MCMXCIV

Definition by Meridian-Webster Dictionary

www.inspirationalstories.com

http://www.storypick.com

http://www.pravsworld.com

https://en.Wikipedia.org

www.Freeaffirmations.org

www.HuffingtonPost.com

www.AdaliaconfidenceandSuccessblog.com

www.ChineseAffirmations.com

www.AffirmYourLife.blogspot.com

www.TrinityAffirmations.com

www.SecretChanges.com

ABOUT THE AUTHOR

———⊶⊷———

KENNETH W KHRISTIAN IS THE Founder and CEO of Promote Health America. He is a Desert Storm veteran, who spent six years in the US Navy as a medical corpsman, specializing as an orthopedics technician. He now serves with the US Postal Service. He is also an author, motivational speaker, health advocate, coach, and mentor serving the metro Atlanta area. Ken's mission is to help others help themselves by providing knowledge and training. Inspiring people to adopt success strategies that will change how they look at life and achieve their goals and dreams. Ken's primary focus is on adolescent, teens and young adults, but the information is relevant for anyone who wants to rise above personal limitations regarding self-improvement, personal growth, and professional development.

You can contact him at:
kwk1962@hotmail.com
Twitter: @CoachKhristian
LinkedIn: www.linkedin.com/in/KenKhristian